Staffordshire Figures
1780–1840
Volume 1

Myrna Schkolne

Schiffer Publishing Ltd
4880 Lower Valley Road • Atglen, PA 19310

Dedication

Dedicated to the memory of Staffordshire's potters, without whom none of this would have happened.

Other Schiffer Books on Related Subjects:

Staffordshire Figures: History in Earthenware 1740-1900. Adele Kenny & Veronica Moriarty. ISBN: 978-0-7643-1917-4. $59.95

Victorian Staffordshire Figures 1875-1962: Portraits, Decorative & Other Figures, Dogs & Other Animals, Later Reproductions. Adrian & Nicholas Harding. ISBN: 978-0-7643-1799-6. $59.95

Library of Congress Control Number: 2013944801

Cover designed by: Bruce Waters
Type set in Bernhard Modern BT/Arrus BT

ISBN: 978-0-7643-4537-1
Printed in China

Published by Schiffer Publishing, Ltd.
4880 Lower Valley Road
Atglen, PA 19310
Phone: (610) 593-1777; Fax: (610) 593-2002
E-mail: Info@schifferbooks.com

Contents

Acknowledgments

These volumes were compiled with the help of collectors, museums, dealers, and auction houses. Many people have gone to extraordinary lengths to supply photographs, while others have generously allowed me to photograph their collections. Some of these contributors are acknowledged within image captions, but others prefer remaining anonymous.

Three individuals were pivotal in preparing this publication. Andrew Dando and John Howard were enormously supportive and helpful, providing extensive material and endless assistance. Malcolm Hodkinson generously contributed a vast amount of archival material as well as his ground-breaking observations on attributions. Malcolm has pioneered a rigorous scientific approach to attributing figures, and his work is the firm foundation for many of the attributions in this book. It enabled me to develop my own theories, so all mistakes are mine.

I thank everyone who has assisted me or provided material for publication. Above all, I thank my husband Ben. His constant loving patience, practical assistance, and encouragement have made my work possible.

Introduction

This work, the first of four volumes, explores the enormous array of enamel-painted earthenware figures made between 1780 and 1840. These figures are dubbed "Staffordshire" because nearly all of them were manufactured in the Staffordshire Potteries, but some were made in other parts of the United Kingdom. All the figures on these pages are decorated with enamel painting. While under-glazed and color-glazed decorations were also in use at this time, pretty enamel painting was the favored mode of embellishment.

The years 1780 and 1840 mark approximate turning points in the production of earthenware figures. From around 1780, enamel-painted figures emerged as alternatives to porcelain figures for refined homes. After 1840, enamel-painted figures deteriorated in quality, becoming mass-market products suited to even the humblest homes. Change in an industry is evolutionary rather than revolutionary, and so it was with earthenware figures. Before 1780, most figures were creamware and were decorated in under-glaze oxides or colored glazes. But in the 1770s, change was afoot that boded well for the production of fine figures: pearlware—a body that appeared whiter because of its blue-tinged lead glaze—was introduced; and the technique of enameling became more widely understood and applied. As a result, earthenware figures with white bodies decorated in a broad color palette could emulate porcelain. From around 1780, James Neale, Ralph Wood, and Enoch Wood popularized pearlware figures painted with polychrome enamels. Enamel-painted figures were more expensive than other earthenware figures, but by 1790 there was a wide range on the market. As the decades marched on, enamel painting became the standard and preferred technique for decorating figures.

Styles of figures also evolved over time. In the eighteenth century, there was a great revival of interest in the classics, and most figures reflect that enthusiasm. Casts from London cast makers and porcelain figures—many of continental origin—inspired or assisted in the modeling of earthenware neo-classical figures as well as classically attired allegorical figures. Some of these subjects were to continue in production for decades, but after 1800 more contemporary themes came into vogue. Increasingly, everyday people were captured in clay in a pleasantly bucolic way. Such figures are often dubbed "social commentaries" because they portray the people and events of their era. Dandies, musicians, street vendors, and performing animals were just a few of the many depictions of contemporary pastimes that filled potters' kilns. The array of new subjects owed its inspiration to progress in the printing industry. In the eighteenth century, printed images had been costly luxuries, but early nineteenth-century advances in printing and engraving brought a slew of images of everyday scenes to the masses. The resulting "visual awakening" inspired potters to fashion in clay the people and sights of their day. The figures that they wrought capture life that otherwise would have gone unrecorded because photography had not yet been invented.

As figures evolved stylistically, other incremental changes took place. Whereas most figures at the beginning of the period were on square bases, by the end of the period most were on mound bases. Whereas earlier square bases are minimally decorated, later mound bases are well painted and are often strewn with flowers to emulate pastoral settings. In keeping with the ambience, many later figures stand before a bocage. Bocages were used in the eighteenth century, but these early bocages are rather minimal. By the 1820s, bocages had come to resemble full leafy trees adorned with bright flowers. Of course, every figure made in 1820 was not on a mound base before a bocage, but when comparing figures across the time spectrum, a gradual shift is noticeable.

Similarly, enamel colors evolved over time. The earliest enamels are exquisitely delicate and were applied with great care. As the years marched on, enamels ran the gamut—bright, muddy, or pleasantly pretty—and on occasion they were applied quite sloppily. Inevitably, there is enormous variability because standards differed from pot bank to pot bank, but the earliest enamels are quite distinctive. This entire period was one of constant experimentation as manufacturers strove to whiten the clay bodies of their figures. By the mid-nineteenth century, clay would be refined to the point where it yielded white bodies, so glazes could become clear because it was no longer necessary to add cobalt to them to whiten the appearance of bodies.

Industrial turmoil and wage pressures in the 1830s coupled with increasingly affordable porcelain figures placed immense pressure on manufacturers to reduce their production costs. In the 1830s, bocages—requiring dozens of molded parts, meticulous assembly, and careful handling—were phased out. While complex figures continued to be made, simplification was the order of the day. The "flat-back," a minimally decorated figure formed from a two-part mold, was to become the standard in the Victorian era.

Attributions

Who are the men who made the intricate figures collectors prize today? As many as a hundred pot banks probably made figures over the period, but only a handful of potters marked their wares. As a result, the identities of most makers remain a mystery. Figure potters usually acquired molds for major components of figures from specialist mold makers, and these molds might pass from pot bank to pot bank over time. Because competing potters sometimes purchased the same figure molds, the form of a figure alone provides no proof of its origin. On the other hand, simpler molds for decorative components—such as bocage leaves, flowers, and sprigs—were typically modeled in-house, making these embellishments specific to their manufactories. Consequently, such ornamental elements can serve as identifiers that link figures from the same source. This work identifies many of these elements and uses them to classify the motley array of early nineteenth-century figures into Groups of common origin.

Attribution is a mine field. While simple molds are likely to be specific to the products of one manufactory, this is not always the case because plagiarism was rife in that era. For this reason, it is helpful to also observe decorators' marks and house styles of decoration (color palette, the painting of dress patterns and eyes, the script used for titles) as these varied enormously between manufactories. Also, the manner in which bases are fashioned and any distinctive tooling routinely used on figures suggest linkages that assist in attribution. The most reliable attributions are those based on several common features. The human brain perceives subtle consistencies and, with experience, can recognize figures as being related to each other in much the same way as it recognizes family relationships in human faces. But it must be stressed that any family of figures assembled on these principles is a hypothesis rather than a certainty, and an attribution will have to be adjusted if new examples point to a different conclusion.

This work attributes a great many figures to known makers. Where a sizable number of figures share common features but their maker's name is unknown, the "Group" has been given a descriptive title. Other figures with shared features have been observed, but, as it is not yet possible to classify these figures into Groups, significant characteristics have been noted in the captions to assist future researchers. Throughout this work, the captions pinpoint salient features pertaining to the attributions, but they cannot possibly detail the many variables validating each attribution.

The shapes of leaves and flowers are critical to attribution, and a basic terminology is used to describe them throughout this work. A simple little leaf is termed a leaf or leaflet, but when joined with others the compound structure becomes a frond. Figure A shows typical leaves and fronds. Frond 1 is a five-leaflet frond. Frond 2 comprises one leaflet atop five others. Some leaves and leaflets are specific in shape. Thus, frond 3 is a single frond comprising three oak leaves, while frond 4 comprises three hawthorn leaves. Fronds can be quite complex, but breaking them down to their smallest component is clarifying. Frond 5 is a fern frond comprising seven tiny leaflets. This is in contrast to frond 6, where the fern frond comprises only three leaflets. Leaf 7 is a single cilantro leaf. Leaf 8 is an anthemion-type leaf, and two leaves are illustrated alongside each other. With this terminology in place, other terms should be self-explanatory.

After centuries of endeavor, the classification of the natural world still requires constant amendment. This work is a first attempt at classifying early figures. As such, it must be subject to constant scrutiny and modification.

Figure A. Basic bocage forms: *1.* Five-leaflet frond. *2.* Frond with one leaflet atop five. *3.* Three oak leaflets in a frond. *4.* Three hawthorn leaves in a frond. *5.* A frond comprising seven fern leaflets. *6.* A frond comprising three fern leaflets. *7.* A cilantro leaf. *8.* Two anthemion leaves.

Values

This work uses the following scale as an approximation of value.

Price A: Up to $1,000 (£625)
Price B: $1,001–$3,000 (£626–£1,875)
Price C: $3,001–$6,000 (£1,876–£3,750)
Price D: $6,001–$9,000 (£3,751–£5,626)
Price E: $9,001–$15,000 (£5,626–£9,375)
Price F: $15,001–$25,000 (£9,376–£15,625
Price G: $25,001 & over (£15,626 & above)

The value of a figure is a function of the standard of its modeling and decoration, its condition, its scarcity, and the appeal of the subject. Essentially, value is quirky, and it can be somewhat subjective. Many small figures are highly desirable and difficult to procure, yet they fall into Price A—even though collectors value them more highly than mediocre figures in higher price brackets.

The determinants of value are not apparent from a photograph, and seemingly identical figures may have vastly different values. The values indicated in captions are not auction values or resale values. Rather, they are the values of figures purchased from a reputable retail source. In each case, the value is an estimate of the value of the figure illustrated. A very similar figure may be worth significantly more or less, depending on the condition and the quality of the glazes and enamels. At the same time, condition issues are not always apparent in a photograph, and, out of respect for those supplying photographs of their treasures for this work, condition reports have not been attached to captions. For that reason, condition is only factored into the value equation to the extent that issues are apparent in the photograph or are known to the author.

Makers and Related Groups

1. John Dale
(active by 1818–1838)

Around 1800, John Dale was, unfortunately, a common name. At least six John Dales were baptized at Stoke and Norton-on-the-Moors between 1776 and 1798. Any one of these might have grown up to be John Dale, the Burslem potter. But the most likely candidate comes from an established family of earthenware manufacturers.[1] His grandfather was probably John Dale (d. 1803), a Cobridge earthenware manufacturer in the partnership of Stevenson, Dale, & Godwin. His father was William Dale, established as an earthenware manufacturer in Cobridge by 1800 and married to Mary Buxton Dale. At his death in 1826, William Dale, by then an earthenware manufacturer in Lane End, left assets shy of £2,000—and a son named John (baptized in Stoke on August 19, 1786). This John Dale is probably our potter because he was a master potter—and at his death in 1838 he was survived by a daughter, named Catherine Buxton Dale—in all likelihood named for Mary Buxton, her paternal grandmother and the wife of William Dale (fig. 1.2).

John Dale was established as an earthenware manufacturer by 1820. *Parson & Bradshaw's Directory* of 1818 lists John Dale as a "china &c manufacturer" residing at Stoke. The *Staffordshire Advertiser* records that in 1819 John Dale withdrew from a china manufacturing partnership with Joseph Paulson; in 1825, John Dale, earthenware manufacturer, married a Miss Walker in Burslem; and in January/February 1838 John Dale, earthenware manufacturer residing at Lane End, died. The will of John Dale, potter, filed in April 1839, records assets valued at less than £200. These were left "for the use and benefit of my dearly beloved wife Jane Dale and our two children of the names of John Morland Dale and Catherine Buxton Dale." Trustees were "my dearly beloved brother Joseph Dale" and William Hopwood (married to John Dale's sister, Hannah).

All Dale figures appear to predate 1835. In June 1841, a two-oven yellow-ware pot bank belonging to John Dale, deceased, was advertised for sale. Perhaps in later years John Dale manufactured yellow wares in lieu of—or in addition to—earthenware figures. Or perhaps this was yet another John Dale!

Figure 1.1. Mercury. Impressed "I. DALE BURSLEM". H: 10". © *Christie's Images Limited 2013.*

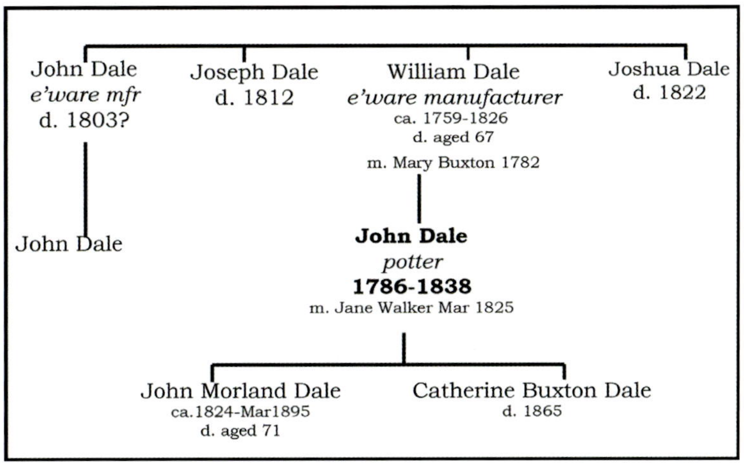

Figure 1.2. John Dale's family tree.

The impressed mark "I. DALE BURSLEM" is found on the reverse of figures. The letter "I" is used for "J". Usually there is a period after the "I", but sometimes there is not (fig. 1.3).

Figure 1.3. John Dale's mark.

Three leaf forms occur on Dale bocages (fig. 1.4). None is exclusive to Dale, so none is particularly helpful in attribution.

1. Five-leaflet frond. This is the only frond form recorded on marked figures.
2. Seven-leaflet fern frond. Sometimes the leaflets have blunt tips. Such fronds occur on figures confidently attributed to Dale, but other potters also used fronds of this form.
3. Three-leaflet frond. These fronds occur on figures attributable to Dale, but they are not exclusive to Dale.

Figure 1.4. Dale bocage frond forms: *1.* Five-leaflet frond. *2.* Seven-leaflet fern frond. *3.* Three-leaflet frond.

Specific flower types occur on Dale figures (fig. 1.5). The flowers are sometimes strewn on bases.

1. Eight-petalled flower. This flower is confined to marked Dale figures and to figures attributable to Dale. The form of the flower is quite specific, and this flower should not be confused with other eight-petalled flowers.
2. Twelve-petalled flower, with alternating long and short petals. This flower otherwise occurs only on three marked Tittensor figures.
3. Six-petalled flower with splayed, gently rounded petals. Other potters used very similar flowers. The Dale flower is generally larger and more splayed. At best, its presence strengthens an argument for a Dale attribution.

Three sprig forms found on marked Dale figures are potential identifiers of Dale's work. All appear to be specific to Dale (fig. 1.6).

1. Fat, five-petalled flower with three leaves. Typically this sprig measures about 1.2" across. A similar but significantly smaller sprig is recorded on a sheep that does not link to Dale.
2. Sprig formed as a bunch of grapes with leaves.
3. Sprig formed as an eight-petalled flower with a stalk and leaves. The flower is like Dale's bocage flower, but it is larger (about 0.6" across). Two floral sprigs of this form are recorded on a sheep impressed "SELMAN" shown in this work. It has not been possible to measure these sprigs to compare sizes.

Figure 1.5. Dale flower forms: *1.* Eight-petalled flower. *2.* Twelve-petalled flower with alternating long and short petals. *3.* Six-petalled flower with splayed, gently rounded petals.

Figure 1.6. Floral sprigs exclusive to Dale: *1.* Five-petalled flower with three leaves. *2.* Bunch of grapes with leaves. *3.* Eight-petalled flower with stalk and leaves.

Bocages that insert into a socket—rather like a candle into a candlestick—are rare, and they appear to be a Dale feature, or perhaps even a Dale innovation (fig. 1.7). This clever technique enabled the vulnerable bocage to be made independently of the rest of the figure. If the bocage was damaged in manufacture, all was not lost, and only the damaged bocage had to be remade. Sometimes the heat of the last firing melded the enamels in the socket, securing the bocage in place. The author has recorded only one figure with a bocage socket that exhibits no other Dale features.

Figure 1.7. Cow with detachable bocage. Attributed to Dale. H: ~5". *Andrew Dando Antiques.*

The author has recorded twelve marked Dale figure forms and one marked bust. The figures display eye-catching features that are helpful in attributing unmarked figures. Most marked figures have pleasingly plump, almost-square faces. Their bases can be attention-grabbing and are often painted in bright yellow-green, with rows of tooled depressions, rather like the teeth marks resulting from pressing a comb into clay, on all sides. Large, bright sprigs, or flowers may be applied to bases. Spill vases, when present, have sharply jagged edges. None of these features is exclusive to Dale, but each is helpful in attributing unmarked figures (fig. 1.8).

Figure 1.8. Pastoral spill vase. Attributed to Dale. H: 7.6". Note the comb marks on the base, the yellow-green enamel, and the jagged vase edges. The largest floral sprigs are exclusive to Dale. *Elinor Penna.*

2. Dudson Family
(active from 1800)

Figure 2.1. *Shepherd.* Attributed to Dudson. H: ~12.5". *John Howard; www.antiquepottery.co.uk.*

The Dudson pot bank has operated as a family business from its foundation to the present day. In 1800, Richard Dudson established his first works at Broad Street, Shelton, and in 1810, he set up a second manufactory on Hope Street under the supervision of his son, Thomas. From about 1815, the Hope Street works made figures along with its other wares.[1] Figure production increased in the 1820s, and by 1830 Dudson was a specialist figure manufactory, although contemporary trade directories fail to list it as such.[2] Twentieth-century excavations at the Hope Street site revealed enamel-painted bocage shards.[3] These have been invaluable in formulating this hypothesis linking figures to Dudson.[4]

Figure 2.2. Dudson bocage frond forms: *1.* Four-leaflet frond, represented by a shard from the Dudson site and two examples from figures. *2.* Five-leaflet frond. *3.* Frond with one leaflet atop seven others.

Dudson bocages use the following fronds, all comprising leaflets of the same form (fig. 2.2).

1. Four-leaflet frond. Four leaflets are arranged rather asymmetrically with one leaflet atop three others. The arrangement of leaflets varies, but the leaflets always match those on the excavated Dudson shard, and a degree of asymmetry in their assembly gives bocages a jumbled, naturalistic look. Hitherto, such bocage fronds have only been recorded on figures attributable to Dudson.
2. Five-leaflet frond. This frond is very similar to the four-leaflet frond, but it has five asymmetrically arranged leaflets rather than four. It is also believed to be specific to Dudson.
3. Frond with one leaflet atop seven leaflets. This frond is larger than the others. Dudson used this frond often, but other potters used it too.

Dudson bocage flowers are small, are often raised on short stalks, and are usually a mixture of several forms. Flower petals are generally red or blue, and yellow was not routinely used. An x-shaped sprig is particularly helpful in identifying Dudson figures. The sprig comprises four leaflets arranged as a cross, often with a central stalked flower. This sprig is believed to be specific to Dudson (fig. 2.3).

Square bases on Dudson figures are often painted brown, black, or black-marbled; otherwise, they have a single brown or black line. Undersides of bases usually show angular rather than rounded corners, but bases of larger figures are the exception. Titles, when present, are in a very recognizable script that is highly suggestive, albeit not definitive, of a Dudson attribution. The most distinctive letters are lower case *g, h, p, t,* and *y*. Titles are painted above a single brown or black line or, when the base is painted black or brown, within an oblong unpainted area (fig. 2.4). Dudson enamels are generally rich and strongly colored with a high gloss. Glazes are usually yellowish rather than blue-tinged.

Figure 2.3. *Left:* the x-sprig that is specific to Dudson figures. *Right:* a Dudson shard with flowers.

Figure 2.4. Distinctively titled Dudson bases.

3. Edge & Grocott
(active circa 1830)

The paucity of marked Edge & Grocott figures coupled with the fact that early trade directories do not list the partnership suggests that the Edge & Grocott venture was short-lived. Reginald Haggar submits that the partnership involved a brief association between Samuel Grocott and either Timothy or Daniel Edge. Samuel Grocott is recorded as an earthenware toy maker in Tunstall from 1822 to 1828, and Daniel Edge made fine china toys in Burslem from 1830–1842.[1] Perhaps their brief partnership occupied the intervening period from around 1828 to 1830. Timothy Edge potted in Burslem around 1840 and is unlikely to have been of the Edge & Grocott partnership, but perhaps William Edge (listed in *Pigot's Directory* as potting in Golden Hill in 1830–31) was involved with the partnership in some way.

Figure 3.1. Boy with bird's nest; shepherd. *Left:* impressed "EDGE & GROCOTT" on a ribbon. *Right:* poorly impressed on a ribbon of the same shape. H: ~5.8" each. The bases of both figures are from the same molds. The shepherd has a restored bocage.

Edge & Grocott figures are marked on a ribbon with canted corners applied to the back of the base. "EDGE & GROCOTT" is impressed on the ribbon (fig. 3.2). Bases are shaped distinctively, and bases of this shape are only recorded on figures made by Edge & Grocott.

The author has recorded five marked figures associated with Edge & Grocott. All have bases of precisely the same shape. Two—a putto with a basket and a boy with a bird's nest—are glazed but unpainted. They are both well marked and stylistically very similar to figures with generic five-leaflet bocages made by Walton, Salt, and others. Three figures are enamel-painted and indecipherably marked on a ribbon with canted corners. Despite the poorly impressed mark, the unusual shape of their bases coupled with the presence of the distinctively shaped ribbon leaves no doubt as to attribution. Two of the figures are a shepherd with a dog, while the third figure portrays a boy holding a dog. Note that the unpainted figure of a putto holding a basket is known from an additional enamel-painted example. That figure appeared in a Dublin exhibition in 1911, but its location is now unknown.[2]

Figure 3.2. The Edge & Grocott marks on the figures in figure 3.1. The enamel-painted figure's mark is indecipherable.

4. Samuel Hall
(active by 1818–1854)

Figure 4.1. Ram. Impressed "HALL". H: 5.8". *Eileen and Robert Carde.*

Figure 4.2. Examples of Samuel Hall's mark.

Hall marked his name in two ways (fig. 4.2). The more common mark is impressed "HALL" on a simple rectangular ribbon. The ribbon may be unpainted, but it is usually painted green, and the impressed letters may use either a large or small font. Less commonly, the mark is impressed directly into the back of the figure, and there is no ribbon.

The author has recorded twenty-six figures marked "HALL". While older literature supposes that Ralph Hall is the potter in question, it seems likely that Samuel Hall manufactured these figures. Samuel Hall was active by 1818 and was still making figures in the 1850s. The relative rarity of marked figures despite his decades of potting activity suggests that Hall produced many unmarked figures.

Samuel Hall was born in 1784. He is first listed in *Pigot's Directory* of 1818 as a potter at New Hall Street, Shelton. By 1822, Hall was proprietor of his own manufactory at this location, for *Allbut's Directory* of 1822 lists him as an earthenware toy manufacturer. Directories for 1830 and 1834 confirm that Samuel Hall focused on figure manufacture, but by the latter date output included "china" figures—probably Parian—in addition to earthenware examples. By 1846, Hall was located at Marsh Street, Shelton, where he manufactured china wares only.[1] In 1854, a final directory entry records Hall as a Parian manufacturer. Hall seems to have retired shortly thereafter—he does not appear in successive directories—and he died on December 29, 1863, aged 79.

Samuel Hall should not be confused with John and Ralph Hall, who potted from circa 1800 and are best known for transfer-printed dinner wares made for the export market. The Halls operated at both Swan Bank, Tunstall, and at the Sitch Pottery, Burslem.[2] In January 1822, they dissolved their partnership.[3] Ralph Hall continued at Tunstall. John Hall, along with his sons, continued at Burslem, but he was bankrupt by 1832 and died in 1838. There is no indication that either Ralph or John Hall potted figures.

Hall bocages use the following fronds (fig. 4.3).

1. Five-leaflet frond. So many other pot banks also used this frond that its presence is no guide to attribution.
2. Seven-leaflet fern frond. This frond form is recorded on only two pairs of marked sheep. Many pot banks used similar fronds, so bocages with these fronds are not helpful in identifying Hall figures.
3. Three oak leaflets in a frond. This is the most helpful frond for identifying Hall figures. Enoch Wood, Salt, "Sherratt," and Hall used such fronds, but Hall's fronds are potted in a distinctive way. Hall tooled the backs of the leaves to emphasize the grooves alongside each central vein, and he painted the acorns on the fronts of the leaves in red, blue, or yellow. This very distinctive combination of features is suggestive of a Hall attribution.

Figure 4.3. Hall's bocage frond forms: *1*. Five-leaflet frond. *2*. Seven-leaflet fern frond. *3*. Three oak leaflets in a frond, with both the front and back of the frond shown. Note that the central vein on the back of each leaf has been tooled for emphasis.

As noted, Hall's oak-leaf bocages include acorns on the fronts of fronds. Unlike typical bocage flowers, the acorns are not modeled separately and applied to the leaves. Rather, they are integral to the structure of the leaves. When painted, each small blob simulates a flower of sorts. Note that acorns appear only on the fronts of fronds. This means that different molds were used for the backs of fronds. In addition, the following separately modeled flower forms occur on marked Hall figures (fig. 4.4).

1. Six-petalled flower. This flower is a powerful pointer that seems to occur only on figures that can be attributed to Hall. The example shown is on the base of a marked ewe.
2. Cup-like flower with seven petals. This flower has been noted on the bases and bocages of marked figures. It is a helpful feature, although it is probably not unique to Hall.
3. Carnation. Most marked figures have the carnations that several pot banks used. The carnations may each be painted in a single color, but sometimes each is painted either red or blue with a noticeably large yellow center. Although not a unique attribute, these eye-catching carnations may provide guidance in combination with other recognized features.
4. Cluster of three tiny flowers with eight pointed petals. This cluster is recorded on four marked sheep, and it appears to be a distinctive feature that may lead to the attribution of further unmarked Hall figures.
5. Star-like flower with six petals. Hall's flower is larger than the small, six-petalled flowers found in multiples on many bocages. The petals can be pointed to such a degree that the flower resembles a star. The flower shown is from a marked Hall figure of Elijah. This flower seems to be specific to Hall.

Although Hall's figures lack the attention to detail of Walton figures or the naïveté of "Sherratt" handiwork, they exude a folksy appeal that charms. Sheep are the commonest figures, and Hall sheep are particularly distinctive and attractive. Usually the coat is deeply channeled with vertical ridges running down the body and horizontal ridges across the chest. Large ears and horns are modeled as one. And, as a farmer pointed out, Hall sheep have distinctively large hind quarters. In short, you can pick a Hall sheep out of a flock with ease. Its bemused expression is as comical today as it was almost two centuries ago.

Figure 4.4. Hall's flower forms: *1*. Six-petalled flower. *2*. Cup-like flower with seven petals. *3*. Carnation. *4*. Cluster of three tiny flowers with eight pointed petals. *5*. Star-like flower with six pointed petals.

5. Lakin & Poole
(active 1791–1795)

In 1791, Thomas Lakin and John Ellison Poole formed a partnership to operate a Burslem earthenware manufactory.[1] Poole supplied the capital, Lakin travelled, and the men hired Thomas Heath to manage their works.[2] Lakin and Poole's billhead emphasized tablewares, with no mention of figures.[3] In February 1795, Thomas Shrigley (Poole's brother-in-law) joined the partnership, which thenceforth operated as Poole, Lakin, and Shrigley.[4] Lakin withdrew from the partnership in January 1796. The *Staffordshire Advertiser* of May 1797 reports the bankruptcy of Poole and Shrigley, and multiple subsequent reports detail the disposal of the works and its stock.[5]

The partnership of Lakin and Poole lasted fewer than five years, but Thomas Lakin remained active in the Potteries for much of the rest of his life. He established a pot bank at Bourne's Bank (or Burn's Bank) in Burslem, but by 1799 it was for sale. Lakin continued seeking work in the Potteries as "a person knowing china, colours, gold, glass, management," but he was bankrupt by 1817 and he died around 1823.[6] In 1824, his impoverished widow published a book of his recipes for preparing and using colors in the manufacture of porcelain, earthenware, and stone china.[7]

Figure 5.2. Details of bases of marked Lakin & Poole figures showing the mark, the scored internal corners that commonly occur, and the recessed upper edge found on larger bases.

Figure 5.1. *The Afsafsination of MARAT, by CHARLOTTE CORDE of Caen, in Normandy. 1793.* Impressed "LAKIN & POOLE". H: 13.6". *Bonhams.*

Lakin & Poole figures may be impressed "LAKIN & POOLE" or "LAKIN. & POOLE" beneath their bases (fig. 5.2). Titles are carefully painted in uppercase letters within a box. This mode of titling seems to be specific to Lakin & Poole. Other than the base of the bocage group noted below, bases are square or rectangular, and larger bases have a slightly recessed upper edge. Many bases have rounded internal corners, but some have internal corners that appear to have been cut with a knife (fig. 5.2). Some marked Neale figures and most Brown Base Group figures also have these distinctive corners.

Lakin & Poole figures are generally made without bocages. However, the author has recorded a single marked group of Cupid and Psyche on a naturalist mound with a simple bocage of paired and single leaves,[8] as well as three unmarked copies of the same group (fig. 5.3). In one instance, the mound is atop a typical Lakin & Poole square base with cut internal corners.

Lakin & Poole figures are uncommon. The figures are painted with delicate colors, and their square bases are usually finely marbled. The faces of marked figures share a strong resemblance, and all have slightly bulging eyes and receding chins. The figures are quite distinctive, and closely similar unmarked examples can be attributed to Lakin & Poole with confidence.

Figure 5.3. Cupid and Psyche. Attributed to Lakin & Poole. H: 9.8". A group just like this one and impressed "LAKIN & POOLE" is recorded.

The author has recorded the following titled Lakin & Poole figures:
Cephalus & Procris,
Rinaldo & Armida, and
The Afsassination of Marat.
Untitled figures include Apollo,[9] Ganymede, Time clipping the wings of Love, Cupid and Psyche (with bocage), and Ariadne. The identity of Ariadne is confirmed by a titled but unmarked look-alike.[10]

An unmarked figure of *Urania* is confidently attributed to Lakin & Poole. Also, an unmarked figure of Minerva that may have been made by Lakin and Poole or by the Brown Base Group is discussed in chapter 18.

6. Leeds Pottery
(active 1790–1820)

Figure 6.1. Figure of a lady. Impressed "LEEDS POTTERY". H: ~8".

The Leeds Pottery in Yorkshire was built in around 1770 and was initially operated by Richard Humble and John and Joshua Green. William Hartley joined the partnership, and in 1781 it was renamed Hartley, Greens, & Co., the "& Co." reflecting the ownership of several other gentlemen. The enterprise was initially very successful, but, with the death and retirement of the partners, decline set in, and in 1820 the manufactory closed.

The Leeds Pottery is better known for its wares than its figures, but a range of figures was made. Subjects suggest that Leeds figures date from the eighteenth century. Marked figures have "LEEDS POTTERY" impressed in uppercase letters, with a dot, dash, or asterisk sometimes separating the words.[1] More commonly, figures are unmarked, but facial features can be distinctive and are notable for receding chins. Most figures stand on square bases that are integral to the figure itself. No examples with bocages are recorded, but in some instances leaves are placed on the support behind the figure, as in figure 6.1.

Between 1890 and 1957, J. W. & G. W. Senior made figures from the old Leeds molds. These too can bear the impressed "LEEDS POTTERY" mark, but their modeling and coloring betray their later date of manufacture.

7. Neale & Co. and Wilson
(active 1778–1817)

Perhaps the figures described as "Neale" should, even when marked, be credited to the Wilson family, for James Neale (1740–1814) was a London merchant rather than an active potter. For a brief period, he was the sole owner of the Church Works, the manufactory that produced the so-called "Neale" figures, while the Wilson family's activities spanned that period and beyond.

In 1762, James Neale, a young London merchant, married Hannah Heath, the daughter of an old Staffordshire family. Hannah Neale's brother-in-law was the Staffordshire potter Humphrey Palmer, and James Neale distributed earthenware products for Palmer and other Staffordshire potters from his successful London emporium. But in March 1778, Humphrey Palmer's financial woes forced him to surrender all his property, including his Church Works pot bank to his principal creditor, James Neale.[1]

Fortunately, the Church Works had an able manager named Robert Wilson, and, after spending a while in Staffordshire sorting out his newly acquired manufactory, Neale was perhaps back in London by 1781,[2] and there he continued distributing the wares of the Church Works, just as he had prior to owning it. Robert Wilson soon became a partner in the Church Works, and the joint ownership of "Neale & Wilson" is documented by an invoice dated November 10, 1783[3], and by an impressed "Neale & Wilson" mark on some wares.[4] On February 27, 1789, James Neale sold the Church Works to Robert Wilson.[5] Neale and Wilson retained an association of sorts because a document dated April 24, 1792, records that the "Copartnership between James Neale and Robert Wilson expired this Day."[6] James Neale continued operating his London emporium, but his direct involvement in manufacture ended.

Robert Wilson was an entrepreneurial potter. Left to his own, he expanded the Church Works. When he died in January 1801, ownership of the Church Works went to his brother, David Wilson. Robert and David had worked together for many years, and at the time of David's death in June 1816, the *Staffordshire Advertiser* noted that the brothers were "together near 50 years e'ware mfrs."[7]

David Wilson's sons, John (Jack) and James, joined their father in 1809 to form David Wilson and Sons. James died in 1814, and the business was then renamed David Wilson and Son. John was a hellion, so by 1816 David Wilson wanted to dissolve their partnership. Death did it for him on June 21, 1816.[8] By July 1817, John Wilson was bankrupt, and the Church Works was sold to satisfy creditors.[9]

The Church Works spanned the lives of Humphrey Palmer, James Neale, Robert Wilson, and David Wilson, and is known more for its wares than its figures. There is no indication that Palmer made enamel-painted figures. Such figures were first made after Neale assumed ownership, i.e., after 1778, and their manufacture probably continued until 1817.

Figure 7.1. A piper, Pomona, and Prudence, each impressed beneath "NEALE & Co". H: 8" max.

The Church Works used varying marks after 1778, but only two marks are known on enamel-painted figures (fig. 7.2). The first mark, an impressed "NEALE & Co" mark, was probably used from around 1780. The "& Co" reflects the financial involvement of one or more of Neale's London partners—and possibly Robert Wilson—in the Church Works. The second mark, an impressed "G" beneath an impressed crown, is known to be the Wilson mark because some wares have "WILSON" impressed alongside this mark. This mark could indicate any point in the Wilson period of 1792–1817. Robert Wilson used this mark, but David Wilson probably continued using it after Robert's death in 1801. In the absence of a mark, it is virtually impossible to attribute or distinguish between Neale and Wilson figures formed from the same molds (fig. 7.3).

Marked Neale & Co figures are consistently particularly refined. The molds are crisp, the glaze has a silky sheen, and the exceptionally pretty, delicate enamels are applied with meticulous care. The color palette routinely uses a lovely turquoise coupled with shades of pink and puce. At their finest, Neale enamels are unsurpassed by those of any other Potteries manufacturer.

Figures marked for either Neale or Wilson most commonly stand on stepped square bases edged in pink or puce (fig. 7.1). The painted line may be at the top or bottom of the stepped area. Figures with the Wilson mark also occur with a blue line. Small figures (Apollo, Ceres, figures depicting the Seasons) customarily stand on a mound with rococo scrolls atop a square base. From beneath, bases are formed in various manners. Often, the rounded internal corners of square bases have been scored with a knife (fig. 7.2).

The author has recorded the following marked Neale/Wilson enamel-painted figure forms:

> **With the Neale mark:** Apollo, Ceres, Spring, Summer, Winter, Autumn, Minerva, Pomona, Actaeon,[10] Venus, Bacchus, Prudence, a piper and a lady playing the tambourine (a pair), Cleopatra, a bust of the Rev. George Whitefield, a shepherdess holding a floral garland before a vase, and two figures flanking a plinth surmounted by a vase.
>
> **With the Wilson mark:** Apollo, Ceres, Spring, Summer, Autumn, and Winter.

Both Neale and Wilson impressed the identity of some smaller figures beneath their bases. In particular, Apollo, Ceres, Spring, Summer, Autumn, and Winter routinely occur so titled. Titled figures may be marked or unmarked. Marked Neale figures can be indistinguishable from their Wilson counterparts, but the Neale figure of Summer always seems to have a black dot painted on the hat brim, whereas similar Wilson figures lack this dot.

Figure 7.3. *CERES*. H: 6". *Left*: marked "Neale & Co". *Center*: unmarked. *Right*: marked for Wilson with "C" (intended to be "G") and a crown. All have *CERES* impressed beneath. *Right: © Fitzwilliam Museum, Cambridge.*

Figure 7.2. *Left, center:* the impressed "NEALE & Co" mark. *Right:* the impressed Wilson mark of a crown above a "G". In two instances, the titles of the figures are also evident.

8. Ralph Salt
(active prior to 1816–1841)

Ralph Salt was born around 1784. He married his wife, Rosannah, at Norton-on-the-Moors on February 16, 1807. Salt is first recorded in partnership with Charles Massey and Joseph Gould, lusterers, on New Street, Hanley, but by May 1816 that partnership had dissolved.[1] Manor court records for April 16, 1817, show that "Ralph Salt, of Shelton, Potter" bought a plot of land from the New Hall estate for £14.[2] *Allbut's Directory* of 1822 lists Ralph Salt as a "lusterer and enameller" at Miles Bank, Hanley. *Pigot's Directory* (1828 and 1830) records Ralph Salt as an earthenware manufacturer, "toy only," at Marsh Street Shelton, and Salt was to remain at this location for the rest of his career. *White's Directory* of 1834 lists Salt among "China & Earthenware Toy Manufacturers," noting that he made "figures & porcelain tablets." This is the first indication that Salt was engaged in porcelain production. In both 1835 and 1841, *Pigot's Directory* lists Salt in the category of "Toy & Ornamental China Manufacturers." On April 17, 1841, *The Staffordshire Advertiser* reported the auction of Ralph Salt's "houses & toy figure warehouse, March St."[3] Probably illness caused Salt to abandon his trade, because he died on November 21, 1846, aged 62.[4]

Today, porcelain figures marked "SALT" occur, but earthenware examples far outnumber them. Most of Salt's figures occupied the "cheap and cheerful" end of the market, and his largest figures are medium-sized deer and apostles. None of his figures is original in concept, and many utilize molds exactly like or closely similar to those of sundry other potters.

The Salt mark occurs in three forms (fig. 8.2). Most commonly, "SALT" is impressed in uppercase serif letters on a small flag-like ribbon applied to the back of the base. Alternatively, "SALT" in serif letters is impressed directly into the back of the base, and not all examples of this mark use the same letter size. One instance of the third form of mark is recorded: "SALT" is impressed in smaller serif letters onto a little parallelogram-shaped ribbon on the back of the base of a deer. Because closely matching pairs of figures with one marked and the other unmarked occur, it seems that not all Salt figures were marked.

Figure 8.2. The three forms of Ralph Salt's mark.

Figure 8.3. Salt's bocage leaf and frond forms: *1.* Five-leaflet frond. *2.* Hawthorn leaf. *3.* Three oak leaves, shown first without an acorn and then with an acorn just visible immediately below the red carnation.

Figure 8.1. *ARCHAR*. Impressed "SALT". H: 6.6"

The clothing on Salt figures is often simply painted. Complex dress patterns are rarely seen, but the edges of skirts are quite frequently painted with a distinctive flame-like design (fig. 8.4). Although not confined to Salt, this style of painting is very typical of Salt figures. When present on a figure that is similar to marked Salt examples, it raises a realistic possibility that the figure may have been made by Salt.

Three frond forms are recorded on marked Salt bocage figures (fig. 8.3).

1. Five-leaflet frond. Most marked Salt figures have bocages assembled from the five-leaflet fronds used by so many other potters. The flowers on the fronds are always carnations painted in red, pink, or mauve, but not blue. They are often, but not always, mounted on short, thick stalks. These bocage fronds with carnations are indistinguishable from those made by others and so are of no assistance in attributing unmarked figures.
2. Hawthorn leaf. These leaves are deeply notched and have five angular subdivisions. Examples recorded have small five-petalled flowers rather than the carnations Salt favored. Bocages with these leaves and flowers are not specific to Salt.
3. Three oak leaves in a frond. A single frond shaped like three oak leaves often forms the bocage of the smallest marked figures. A carnation is usually applied to the front of the frond. Unmarked figures with precisely this type of bocage and with a carnation applied to the front are quite likely to be by Salt. In some cases, there are little acorns on the front and back of the frond. The acorns are painted green along with the oak leaves. Several other potters also used triple-oak-leaf fronds with acorns, but usually the acorns are painted differently from the leaves and carnations are not present.

Salt figures do not have distinctive bases, but those shown in figure 8.4 are typical. Titles, when present, are almost always impressed and may be emphasized by being painted black. Titles painted in free-hand are known only on two figures of Lubin Log and on one of Paul Pry. In these cases, the titles are painted in iron red in a well-formed cursive script. "Selina" painted in the same hand is noted on the front of the skirt of a single figure of Air.

All known marked Salt figures occur as one of a pair or a set of four. In total, there are only forty recorded marked figure forms, a surprisingly small number for a pot bank that was apparently active for so many years. Perhaps Salt only marked figures for a limited time, and, indeed, marked figures are stylistically typical of the 1820–1835 period. Figures resembling marked Salt figures are all too common. In the case of a well matched pair of figures, one of which is marked and the other is unmarked, it seems reasonable to attribute the unmarked figure to Salt. Otherwise, a Salt attribution of an unmarked figure is dubious at best.

Figure 8.4. Typical skirt patterns and bases on Salt figures.

9. Theophilus Smith
(active circa 1789–1800)

Theophilus Smith was a successful potter who is better remembered for his tragic life than for the figures he made. From 1788, Smith developed a township called Smithfield on a Tunstall estate. The township included a pot works, a flint mill, forty cottages, shops, an inn, and a lavish home for the Smith family. By 1800, Smith was dogged by creditors and he apparently suffered from some mental derangement. In June, Smith shot and tried to stab a Mr. Wainwright. Wainwright, a Liverpool merchant and one of Smith's numerous creditors, was attempting to help Smith allay hostile creditors. After the shooting, Smith fled to London, but he was arrested and sentenced to hanging. His wife visited him in the Stafford jail in January 1801, and Smith shot and killed them both.[1] Smith had been declared bankrupt in 1800. His property was dispersed at auctions in 1800 and 1801.[2]

Theophilus Smith's mark (fig. 9.1), impressed "T. Smith", has been recorded on four figures, all shown in this work: a titled Charity, an untitled Hope, a figure of a boy with a dog, and a figural candlestick with two cherubs clambering up it. Interestingly, the titling on Charity appears to be in the same small, red script routinely associated with Ralph Wood figures. This is the only instance in which this script has been recorded on a figure devoid of Ralph Wood features.

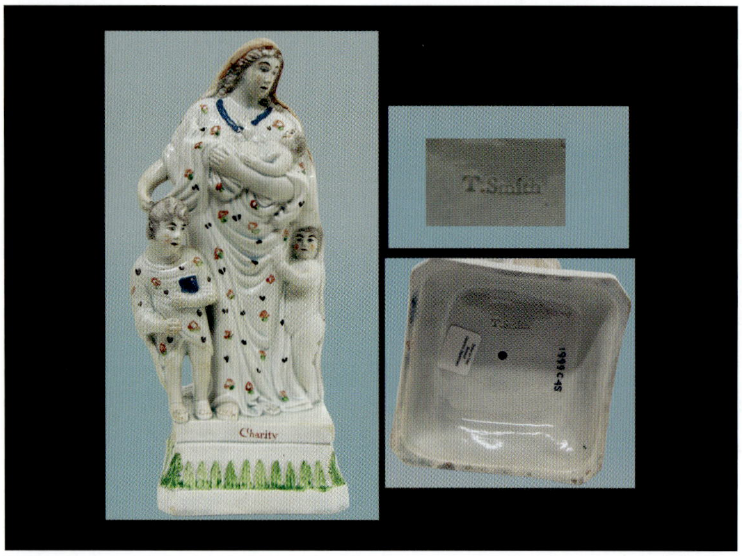

Figure 9.1. *Charity.* Impressed "T. Smith". H: 9.7". *Image courtesy of The Potteries Museum & Art Gallery, Stoke-on-Trent, UK.*

10. Charles Tittensor
(active from circa 1803–1820s)

The Tittensor mark is thought to be that of Charles Tittensor. Notices in the *Staffordshire Advertiser* of February 1802 and October 1803 announce the formation and subsequent dissolution of the Hanley partnership of Robert Pope and Charles Tittensor. Charles Tittensor then entered into a venture with John Tittensor that was dissolved by early 1805.[1] Next, Charles Tittensor was a partner in Tittensor and Simpson, which operated until 1813.[2] *Parsons & Bradshaw's Directory* of 1818 records Charles Tittensor as a "potter" at Queen Street, Shelton, but the directory does not list Tittensor as an earthenware manufacturer. *Allbut's Directory* of 1822 records Tittensor in the same manner,[3] but thereafter he is not listed again. Directories of that day are inaccurate, so it is quite possible that Tittensor continued potting after 1822.

Figure 10.1. Boy reading. Impressed "TITTENSOR". H: 7". Left side of the bocage restored. Tittensor made this same figure decorated in under-glaze colors with a very different bocage.

Marked Tittensor figures are impressed "TITTENSOR" in bold letters (fig. 10.2). They are best known from a small number of quirky examples decorated in under-glaze colors. Such figures have distinctive bocages of a form that has not yet been recorded on enamel-painted figures. Only four marked enamel-painted figures (all shown in this work) are known: a tiny deer, a small Turk, a boy reading, and a man seated with a dog in his lap. The first three figures have bocages. In each case, the bocage leaves are non-specific. The bocage flowers, however, are rather interesting. Each flower comprises twelve petals that alternate from long to short (fig. 10.2). Flowers of precisely this form have only otherwise been recorded on figures marked as made by John Dale and on figures confidently attributed to Dale. In addition, several enamel-painted busts of Czar Alexander I impressed "TITTENSOR" have been noted.

Conclusions about Tittensor are speculative at best. His enamel-painted figures all appear to date from around the 1820s. The marked Tittensor figures of a Turk and a reading boy are recorded decorated in either enamel or under-glaze colors. However, the under-glaze versions have very different bocages. Possibly, Tittensor introduced enamel-painted figures at a slightly later date in his career, using bocages more in keeping with contemporary taste.

Figure 10.2. The Tittensor mark and the flower found on marked Tittensor figures.

11. John Walton
(active circa 1806–1835)

John Walton is believed to be the man behind the Walton mark found on so many figures. Burslem parish records indicate that a John Walton was baptized on February 20, 1780.[1] Reginald Haggar concurs with William Chaffers in concluding that John Walton was a manufacturer by about 1806.[2]

John Walton's name first appears in trade directories in 1818, when "Earthenware Manufacturers in the Potteries" are first listed as a distinct group. By all accounts, by that year Walton was a well-established manufacturer with diverse enterprises. *Parsons & Bradshaw's Directory* of March 1818 lists John Walton both as a "Colour Maker" on Pleasant Street, Burslem, and as an "Earthenware &c. Manufacturer" at Haderage, Burslem. That same year, Walton apparently abandoned color-making to focus on potting, for *Pigot's Directory* of August 1818 records him only as an earthenware manufacturer at a new location: Navigation Road, Burslem.

Walton's figures are his legacy, but he made other wares too. *Allbutt's Directory* of 1822 notes that John Walton made both figures and Egyptian black wares, and *Pigot's Directory* (1828 and 1830) records John Walton as a general earthenware manufacturer. *White's Directory* of 1834 confusingly lists John Walton under both "Egyptian black mfrs. only," and "Toy Manufacturers," but *Pigot's Directory* of 1835 clarifies this by listing John Walton at two Burslem premises: at Navigation Road as a general "Earthenware Manufacturer" and at Waterloo Road as a "Toy and Ornamental China Manufacturer." Apparently, by that time the "toy" or figure business was successful enough to warrant expanding to a dedicated facility at the Waterloo Road location. However, Walton must have stopped working shortly thereafter, for his name does not appear in subsequent directories. In June 1839, the Navigation Road manufactory—a two-oven facility—was auctioned by its then-owner, a bankrupt figure potter of around sixty years of age: Walton's son-in-law, George Hood.[3] The date of John Walton's death is unknown.

The John Walton listed in trade directories may not have been the Walton who manufactured figures with the Walton mark. A Walton mark does not occur on any basalt wares, despite John Walton's recorded production of that black stoneware body. To complicate matters, the names of other Waltons abound in the directories. James Walton, Joseph Walton, and Stephen Walton, all of the Potteries hamlet of Shelton, are described in early-nineteenth-century manorial records as potters[4]—as is John Walton of Burslem.[5] Trade directories of 1830, 1834, 1835, and 1841 record the existence of Joshua Walton, a specialist toy manufacturer in Shelton, yet there is no evidence that Joshua Walton marked any of his figures. However, because the criteria for inclusion in trade directories are not known, and because errors and omissions occurred, the possibility that Joshua Walton—or some other Walton—was potting from an earlier date and was connected in some way with marked Walton figures cannot be dismissed.

Walton produced eighty-four marked figure forms, more than did any other manufacturer of his day.[6] Unfortunately, Walton is generously credited with a prodigious array of unmarked figures. Today, the words "Walton," "Walton-type," and "Walton-school" have become almost synonymous with "bocage figure." As a host of plausible explanations exist for different pot banks producing Walton look-a-likes, attribution of unmarked figures to Walton is seldom likely to be correct.

Figure 11.1. *FRIENDSHIP*. Impressed "WALTON". H: 7.4".

The "WALTON" mark is usually on an elongated ribbon applied on the reverse of bases; on spill vases, the ribbon is sometimes beneath. The impressed letters are uppercase with serifs. Occasionally, the letters (with serifs) are molded in relief on an arc-shaped ribbon. Both versions of the mark are believed to be John Walton's because both can be seen on almost identically formed figures (fig. 11.2).

Figure 11.2. Both forms of John Walton's mark.

Figure 11.3. Walton's bocage leaf and frond forms: *1.* Five-leaflet frond. *2.* Large-broad leaf frond. *3.* Anthemion-like frond. *4.* Rounded anthemion-like leaf. *5.* Three-leaflet frond.

The frond forms comprising the bocages of marked Walton figures also occur on other figures, so none can support an attribution. Five leaf forms occur (fig. 11.3).

1. Five-leaflet frond. This is the most common Walton bocage frond. Sometimes, the fronds are arranged in an arc instead of in a tree form.
2. Large, broad leaf. Such leaves occur on only five marked figure forms. Walton also made these figures with five-leaflet fronds.
3. Anthemion-like frond. These fronds have been recorded on three marked Walton figure forms.
4. Rounded anthemion-like leaf. These leaves have been recorded on only Walton deer, which, strangely, are known from just three virtually identical examples.
5. Three-leaflet frond. The leaflets have pointed tips. These fronds have been recorded on two figures of a cherub of the same form.

Flowers on bocages are of assorted types, none of which is specific to Walton. However, a large rosette in the center of the decorative scrolls on the bases of some figures is specific to marked Walton figures (fig. 11.1). The rosette is molded into the earthenware body. The color it is painted varies.

The following perplexing questions about Walton remain unanswered:

1. Why does a marked Walton *ST. PAUL* occur paired with an unmarked *ST. PETER*? The figures often seem to have been made and decorated as a pair, and they can match in every detail, yet *ST. PAUL* is always marked, but *ST. PETER* never is. All other two-dozen-plus Walton figure pairs routinely have marks on both figures, so it is uncertain whether unmarked examples of *ST. PETER* were indeed made by Walton, although they probably were.

2. Why are there unmarked look-a-likes of some Walton figures, but not of others? Unmarked look-a-likes of Walton sheep can be found, but not unmarked look-a-likes of Walton cows. Similarly, unmarked look-a-likes of Walton bird-nester pairs occur, but not unmarked look-a-likes of Walton showmen or show women. Any subtle differences between marked and unmarked examples are perplexingly inconclusive.

3. Although deer are the most ubiquitous of pearlware figures, only three examples of marked Walton deer are recorded, and all are from the same figure molds.

Figure 11.4. Gardeners groups. Despite their Walton-like appearance, these unmarked groups cannot be attributed to Walton because other manufacturers produced groups with similar features. *Center: Elinor Penna. Right: Saffron Walden Museum.*

4. What of the unmarked gardener groups that appear to be so very Walton-like (fig. 11.4)? These groups only occur with one or the other of the bocage leaf forms used by Walton. Their composition, scale, style, and color palette is reminiscent of other Walton groupings—but these features are also typical of other pearlware figures of the period. Because these gardening groups lack characteristics specific to Walton, and because a marked example has not yet been recorded, they must remain unattributed.

12. Ralph Wedgwood (active 1788–1800)

Most figures marked "Wedgwood" are quite unremarkable, but the identity of their maker is somewhat puzzling. Josiah Wedgwood's name is inextricably associated with earthenware production, but Josiah Wedgwood's manufactory did not produce the figures impressed with his famous name. Because marked Wedgwood figures so closely resemble figures made by other manufacturers, some speculate that other potters made these figures for Josiah Wedgwood and impressed the Wedgwood mark on their work. However, the Wedgwood manufactory's extensive archives reveal no evidence that marked Wedgwood figures were bought. In the absence of proof to the contrary, it must be concluded that figures marked "WEDGWOOD" were made by Josiah Wedgwood's second cousin, Ralph Wedgwood.

Ralph Wedgwood had a brilliant scientific bent. His father, Thomas, had been Josiah Wedgwood's partner, and on Thomas's death in 1788, his son Ralph funded his father's start-up pot bank at the Hill House Works, Burslem. This pot bank was known as Wedgwood & Co., and it was run by Ralph, his brother Samuel, and Peter Swift, formerly an accountant for Josiah Wedgwood.[1] By 1797, Ralph was bankrupt. In January 1798, he joined the Knottingley Pottery, which had been operational since 1793 in Ferrybridge, Yorkshire. The partners were John Foster, John Thompson, John Seaton, and William Tomlinson.[2] Ralph was to manage the works and contribute his knowledge and technical skills, and the partnership was renamed Tomlinson, Foster, Wedgwood & Co. to reflect Ralph's involvement and to capitalize on the famous Wedgwood name. But Ralph's inventive ideas strained the partnership's financial resources, and the agreement was dissolved, with Ralph being paid to leave by January 1, 1801.[3] With that, Ralph Wedgwood's career as a manufacturer ended. Thereafter, he devoted his life to his scientific interests. He invented carbon paper,[4] and by 1815 he had invented the telegraph. At that time, there was no interest in his invention because the government believed that victory at Waterloo had made improved long-distance communications unnecessary.[5]

Figures made by Ralph Wedgwood are impressed "WEDGWOOD" (sometimes with a period afterwards, sometimes not) in small letters (fig. 12.2). The impressed mark "WEDGWOOD & CO" occurs too, but it is less common. The latter mark is believed to date from the Knottingley period of 1798–99, but as both Ralph Wedgwood's operating partnerships were known as "Wedgwood & Co", possibly figures made by both partnerships were marked in this way.

Ralph Wedgwood was a plagiarist extraordinaire, and many of his figures are direct copies of figures made by others. This makes attributing unmarked figures to Wedgwood impossible, and the problem is exacerbated by the fact that Wedgwood's marked figures have no distinguishing features. The following figures marked "WEDGWOOD" are recorded:

A boy and dog paired with a girl and sheep. These also occur with Theophilus Smith's mark.

Prudence and Fortitude. These are indistinguishable from examples made by Wood & Caldwell in this period.

Ariadne. A large classical figure sometimes called "Purity," after similar figures attributed to Wood & Caldwell.

Large figure of Venus, height 29.5".

Eagle on a box base of the type associated with Enoch Wood.

Venus, Neptune, Flora, Faith, Hope, Charity, Lost Coin, Lost Sheep, Apollo, Simon, male hurdy-gurdy player, female lute player, slumbering cherub, and marmot girl. Each of these is on square base banded with a painted line. If titled, the title is impressed in small, uppercase letters. Also, a figure of Adonis is on a square base with a recessed upper edge painted with a line.

Figure 12.1. The struggle of Eros and Anteros. Impressed "WEDGWOOD". H: 16.4". *Angus Northeast.*

Figure 12.2. Ralph Wedgwood's mark.

Cleopatra, titled *CLEOPTRA,* and apparently from the Wood & Caldwell molds.

Bust of Shakespeare and a bust of the Madonna, impressed *SADNESS.*

Pair of recumbent naked infants on marbled bases.

Pair of Medici lions on marbled bases.

Youthful couple standing on a square base banded with a painted line before a bocage (Volume 4, fig. 145.3). This is the only Wedgwood figure with a bocage, and it is known from one example.

Eros and Anteros tussling. A large group recorded on a square base.

In addition, the group of Eros and Anteros also occurs on a round base marked "WEDGWOOD & CO". The author knows of only one other figure with that mark: an unidentified classical maiden, height 19.5", holding her hem with one hand and possibly a plant with the other.

13. Enoch Wood
(active 1783–1840)
and Wood & Caldwell
(1791–1818)

Enoch Wood was born in 1759.[1] His father, Aaron, was a skilled modeler, and Enoch evidenced extraordinary modeling skills at an early age. As a youth, Enoch worked for Josiah Wedgwood before being apprenticed to Humphrey Palmer. In 1783, Enoch left Palmer's manufactory—then owned by James Neale—writing, "I began business for myself Nov. 11th 1783 with partner Ralph Wood for a few weeks only dismiss [*sic*] him with all his things again."[2] Until 1791, Enoch Wood potted independently.

In January 1791, Enoch Wood went into partnership with the lawyer James Caldwell. An entry in James Caldwell's diary reads, "On the 1st day of January 1791 commenced my connection with Mr. Enoch Wood in the manufactury [*sic*] of Earthern Ware [*sic*] & a new set of Works were soon after begun to be erected."[3] Their partnership operated as Wood & Caldwell (with Wood being the working partner and Caldwell providing business expertise and capital), and in its time, it was referred to as Wood & Co.[4] They constructed an extensive manufactory on a large plot of land in the heart of Burslem. It was known as the Fountain Place because the engine that pumped water for the works also operated a pump at the factory gate that gave Burslem a free source of water. Enoch Wood lived on this estate. On July 17, 1818, Enoch Wood bought out James Caldwell's working capital, and their relationship ended on a bitter note.

From August 1818 until 1840, Enoch Wood operated with his sons Enoch, Joseph, and Edward as Enoch Wood & Sons. This enterprise was thought to be the largest exporter of Staffordshire wares to America, and it also ventured into porcelain manufacture.[5] Operations were extensive, occupying three or four manufactories and employing over one thousand people. In 1840, Enoch Wood died, aged 82, and Burslem ground to a halt for a day of mourning. His impact on Potteries' life had been so profound that he was known as "Father of the Potteries." By then, his son Joseph had left the partnership, but the manufactory continued in the hands of his sons Enoch and Edward until its closure in 1846.

The three phases of Enoch Wood's operations utilized varying marks, but none of the marks was used extensively, and nearly all figures are unmarked:

> **1783–1790.** The impressed "E. WOOD" mark was used in this period. It occurs on busts of Homer and Plato and on figures of Prudence, Fortitude, and Demosthenes, all of which appear to predate 1790. The "ENOCH WOOD" mark also seems to have been used in this period. It is recorded on a figural jug[6] and on a pair of busts of Plato and Homer.[7] Identical busts of Plato and Homer are marked "E. WOOD", suggesting that the marks may have been used interchangeably (Volume 4, chapter 200).
>
> **1791–1818.** The impressed "WOOD & CALDWELL" mark was used during the operation of this partnership. This mark is on busts of Wellington (in two sizes), Nelson (bronze glazed), and Czar Alexander, as well as on paired recumbent lions, a large horse with spill vase, a large cow with spill vase, Falstaff, Ceres/Plenty, triton candlesticks, two models of an unclad boy seated on a tree, and a bronze-glazed Virgin and child. In addition to the mark, "Burslem" is sometimes impressed or incised in a large copperplate hand.
>
> **1818–1845.** Three marks are probably from this period: "WOOD" impressed (beneath three examples of Van Dunder); "Enoch Wood & [illegible]" impressed (beneath a Flemish musician); and "E Wood & Sons" incised in large script (beneath a cow and calf before a bocage).

It is possible that the "E. WOOD" and "ENOCH WOOD" marks used in the first period of operation were used thereafter. However, these marks are also found on figures made decades after Enoch Wood's demise. In particular, marked figures of St. Sebastian and busts of Washington occur painted in a manner and in a palette that betray their later manufacture.

Marked figures are relatively easy to date, but unmarked figures are perplexing. There is every reason to suppose that the same figure forms were made whatever the status of the manufactory's legal ownership. Thus, a look-a-like of a marked Wood & Caldwell figure may have been made after 1818 or before 1791. Twentieth-century excavations revealed unmarked figures made by Enoch Wood in the 1820s that are indistinguishable from examples marked "E. WOOD" and "WOOD & CALDWELL".[8]

Enoch Wood shards and figures excavated in the twentieth century reveal a number of distinctive bocage leaves that support or assist in attribution.[9] Ten leaf forms are noted on Enoch Wood bocages (figs. 13.2 and 13.3).

Figure 13.1. Britannia. Impressed "WOOD & CALDWELL" and incised "Burslem". H: 9.3".

Figure 13.3. Enoch Wood bocage fronds: *4.* Seven-leaflet fern frond with matching shard. *5.* Five-leaflet fern frond with matching shard. *6.* Three-leaflet fern frond. *7.* Two-leaflet frond. *8.* Three hawthorn leaves in a frond. *9.* Frond with one leaflet atop four. *10.* Frond with one leaflet atop three. *Shards: Image courtesy of The Potteries Museum & Art Gallery, Stoke-on-Trent, UK.*

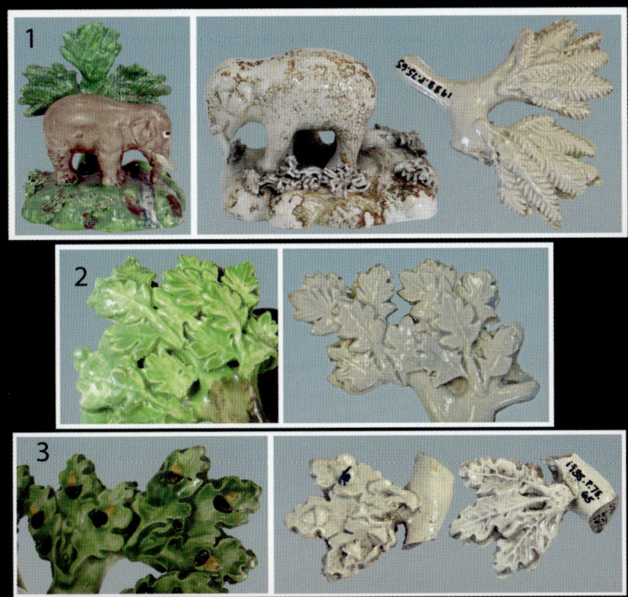

Figure 13.2. Enoch Wood bocage leaves and fronds: *1.* Palm leaf bocage on a small elephant; alongside are matching shards. *2.* Five seven-lobed leaflets in a frond, alongside a matching shard. *3.* Three oak leaflets in a frond, alongside matching shards. *Shards: Image courtesy of The Potteries Museum & Art Gallery, Stoke-on-Trent, UK.*

1. Palm leaf. An uncommon palm-like leaf matches excavated shards. To the author's knowledge, this bocage leaf is only seen on figures attributable to Enoch Wood. Figure 13.2 shows the shard and an excavated figure, along with a complete figure with a palm-leaf bocage.

2. Five seven-lobed leaflets, assembled in a frond. This uncommon frond appears to be specific to Enoch Wood and matches excavated shards.

3. Three oak leaflets in a frond, with acorns on the front of the frond. This frond matches excavated shards, but Enoch Wood used such fronds only occasionally. Other potters made very similar fronds, often also with acorns. However, in the author's experience, Enoch Wood always painted the acorns yellow and the acorn cups brown.

4. Seven-leaflet fern frond. Enoch Wood apparently used this frond more than any other, and it is always accompanied by small six-petalled star flowers arranged singly or in threes. Fronds of this form were excavated, but other potters used very similar fronds and flowers, so attribution must be supported by other Enoch Wood features.

5. Five-leaflet fern frond. This frond is similar to the previous one and also occurs with the small six-petalled flowers that Enoch Wood favored. Several pot banks used this frond, and Enoch Wood used it infrequently. It matches excavated shards.

6. Three-leaflet fern frond. This is a small frond. It is sometimes used with the seven-leaflet fern frond, or it may be used alone on side branches of small figures. Only rarely is it used alone within a main bocage. Again, it occurs with small six-petalled star flowers arranged singly or in threes.

7. Two-leaflet frond. This small frond is occasionally found on figures attributable to Enoch Wood, but other potters used very similar fronds.

8. Three hawthorn leaves in a frond. Bocages using triple-hawthorn fronds occur occasionally and are decorated with small flowers. Other potters used very similar fronds, sometimes with the same flowers.

9. One leaflet atop four others. This frond occurs with six-petalled or eight-petalled flowers and is the second commonest frond on figures attributed to Enoch Wood. Although no shard supports attribution, bocages with this frond appear to be specific to Enoch Wood.

10. One leaflet atop three others. This frond is similar to the previous one and also uses six-petalled or eight-petalled flowers. It may be used alone or in combination with the previous frond within the same bocage. It is not specific to Enoch Wood.

Most Enoch Wood/Wood & Caldwell flowers are small and unremarkable. However, a large four-petalled flower on the bases of some marked figures is exclusive to Enoch Wood/Wood & Caldwell. This flower is helpful in attributing unmarked figures (fig. 13.4).

Figure 13.4. This large flower is specific to Enoch Wood/Wood & Caldwell figures.

A hollow box-type base (closed at the bottom) seems to be specific to Enoch Wood, with one exception: this base occurs on a marked Wedgwood figure of an eagle. As Ralph Wedgwood plagiarized Wood figure forms, his use of this base is not surprising. Ralph Wedgwood was active from 1788 to 1800, so Enoch Wood was probably using this base at that early date (fig. 13.5).

Figure 13.5. Girl with basket on a box base. H: 6.3". This box base is a strong indicator of an Enoch Wood attribution.

Enoch Wood used other bases too. Figures on square bases consistently have undersides with shallow recesses, thick walls, and angular corners. These bases are ordinarily unpainted except for a single red/brown line or two ochre lines. Bases of the Wood & Caldwell period may be painted solid black or in a black marbled design. Some figures have mound bases that are open beneath, and these often have thick walls. Either type of base may have painters' marks and/or impressed numbers and symbols beneath. Such features are useful pointers to an Enoch Wood origin but on their own do not support attribution (fig. 13.6).

The following numbers are recorded impressed beneath bases of figures associated with Enoch Wood: 1 (cherub holding a basket); 2 (man with French horn, Hope); 3 (Charlotte at the tomb of Werther, Hygeia, a cherub holding a basket, pair of boy and girl vendors); 4 (Charity); 6 (Diana); 8 (girl with tambourine, camel); 10 (Charlotte at the tomb of Werther); 12 (recumbent deer, boy emblematic of autumn, man holding large basket); 13 (Prudent Mother, male Turk); 14 (female Turk); 15 (Madonna with child, girl emblematic of spring, shards of bases of figures of Dusty Bob and Billy Waters); 16 (male showman with bugle, seated girl with basket); 18 (male and female figures of Old Age); 19 (Faith, Hope, Charity); 20 (Sam Swipes, Van Dunder, a religious male figure, possibly a disciple); 24 (monk or priest, two different versions in different sizes); 27 (lady with mandolin, sportsman with gun, Nell, Jobson); 30 (lady with tambourine); 32 (a pair of cherubs, each with a basket); and 33 (Iphigenia).

Figure 13.6. Bases of two Enoch Wood figures. The base on the left is impressed "WOOD & CALDWELL". The base on the right is from a small elephant with a palm bocage (matching excavated forms) and is impressed "16". Both bases exhibit painters' marks.

14. Ralph Wood II and Ralph Wood III (active 1782–1801)

Ralph Wood (1748–1795) was born into an illustrious family of potters residing in Burslem, at the heart of the Staffordshire Potteries. He is sometimes referred to as Ralph Wood II because his father, a renowned modeler, was also named Ralph. In 1769, young Ralph Wood was hired by his great-uncles, John and Thomas Wedgwood of the Big House in Burslem.[1] In 1772, Ralph and his brother John set up their own pot bank,[2] but the venture soon failed and the brothers moved to Bristol where they retailed earthenware and glass.[3] In 1776, John returned to Burslem, and Ralph continued running the Bristol shop. The year 1781 was Ralph Wood's *annus horribilis*. He was falsely accused of sodomy, and his goods and possessions were sold to satisfy his creditors.[4] He returned home, and recent research indicates that by August 1782, Ralph was established as a master potter in Burslem.[5] In November 1783, Ralph joined his cousin Enoch in the briefest of partnerships. In the Enoch Wood papers acquired by the Potteries Museum in 2005, Enoch Wood notes, "I began business for myself Nov 11th 1783 with partner Ralph Wood for a few weeks only dismiss [*sic*] him with all his things again." The underlining is Enoch's, but these words relegate to the realm of myth the long-held belief that Ralph Wood was a mere sales manager for Enoch Wood from 1783 to 1789. Instead from 1782, aside for a period of "a few weeks only," Ralph potted independently until his death in 1795. His son, also named Ralph and known as Ralph Wood III, continued as a master potter until he died in 1801, aged 26 years.

Figure 14.1. *Flemifsh Music, Flemifsh Music*. Impressed "Ra. Wood Burslem". H: 8.9" (L), 9.4" (R).

The maker's mark recorded on Ralph Wood's enamel-painted figures is "Ra. Wood Burslem", impressed in a rectangular stamp (fig. 14.2). Less commonly, the mark is shortened to "Ra. Wood".[6] The author has documented the mark on twenty-five enamel-painted figures and busts. An impressed "W" has been observed on ten enamel-painted figures attributed to Ralph Wood, the "W" seemingly indicating Wood.[7]

Ralph Wood made both enamel-painted and color-glazed figures, and a sizable number of these figures have both an impressed mark and a number. For this reason, such numbers are inextricably associated with Ralph Wood. The author has recorded 112 numbers and corresponding enamel-painted figures or busts. These figures and busts display many common features that enable the attribution of additional figures that have neither a mark nor a number. The presence of an impressed number, along with other Ralph Wood characteristics, is a strong Ralph Wood identifier.[8] Human error probably explains why the same number sometimes occurs on very different figure forms, and why different numbers can occur on identical figure forms. The purpose of the numbers remains a mystery, but they do seem to suggest the sequence in which the models were introduced.

Many Ralph Wood figures stand on distinctive square bases. From beneath, bases have gently rounded internal corners.[9] A line is frequently painted around the front and sides of the base but not on the back.[10] An impressed number, when present, is usually on the unpainted back of the base (fig. 14.2). Figures not on square bases usually are painted on all sides of the base, and a number may be impressed anywhere on the base.

Figure 14.2. Ralph Wood bases. *Left*: A base with an impressed mark and gently rounded internal corners. *Right*: The line is painted around only the front and sides of the base, not the back. A number, when present, is usually impressed on the unpainted back surface.

Figure 14.3. Typical titling and painting on the bases of Ralph Wood figures.

Titling on Ralph Wood figures, when present, is in one of the distinctive scripts shown in figure 14.3. With one exception, these scripts are only recorded on Ralph Wood figures.[11]

> Small fine script, nearly always with red letters. This is the most common script. All titled figures with impressed numbers use only this script. The same script also occurs on unnumbered figures attributed to Ralph Wood. On rare occasions, the little letters are all uppercase.
>
> Larger script with red or black letters. This script is a little heavier and may be by a different hand. It occurs on unnumbered figures that are confidently attributed to Ralph Wood. Some of these figures have numbered look-a-likes, titled in small red script.
>
> Larger, heavier black script. Usually the black letters are italicized. This script is found on figures confidently attributed to Ralph Wood. These figures are usually painted in a muddier palette and are thought to have been made at the tail-end of the Ralph Wood era.

Many Ralph Wood figures stand atop mounds, and the mounds are painted in distinctive palettes (fig. 14.3). A rainbow-effect polychrome palette (with dabs of pink, blue, and green) occurs on figures titled in fine red script. At the other end of the spectrum, a muddy green/brown palette occurs on the mounds of figures titled in large black script. There is some middle ground. Mounds in a watery pale green and brown palette occur. These mounds occur on most figures. They may be titled in either manner, but more commonly they are titled with small red letters (figs. 14.1, 14.3).

Because Ralph Wood figures predate the heyday of the bocage, most do not have bocages. When present, bocages are sparse and comprise distinctive leaflets arranged in twos, threes, or fours. The three-leaflet arrangement usually occurs on figures decorated in the small red script, while the four-leaflet arrangement is usually found on figures titled in a large black script. Flowers are the simplest of round forms with minimal attention to petal structure. They are applied to stalks, usually in clusters of threes. The unusually large bocage shown in figure 14.4 is formed in the typical manner.[12]

Ralph Wood figures with marks and/or numbers are believed to be the earliest. These are almost all painted in a delicate palette with fine red titling. Generally, such figures are thought to predate figures painted in a muddier palette and titled in the larger black script. Most of the latter have bocages, supporting the belief that they were later. In addition, a small cluster of enamel-painted stoneware figures (the Four Seasons, Pomona, Ceres, a soldier) display distinct Ralph Wood decoration, including a blue line around three sides of the base and typical titling.[13] Ralph Wood produced both porcelain and earthenware figures, and possibly these stoneware figures were his experimental work.

Stylistically, many Ralph Wood figures are classical or continental in inspiration, reflecting their early date of manufacture. After the demise of Ralph Wood and his son, other potters used or replicated many of the Ralph Wood molds, but their handiwork lacks the fine modeling and enameling that were Ralph Wood characteristics.

Figure 14.4. Bocages on figures of Elijah and the Widow, impressed "169" and "170" respectively. *Angus Northeast.*

The following Ralph Wood figures with impressed numbers have been recorded.[14]

1\. *Gardener*. Male.
2\. Lady holding basket of flowers
4\. & *Partner*. Girl with piglet in box.
5\. Winter/Clown/Sweep. As 6 and 74.
6\. *Clown*. As 5 and 74.
8\. Gardener. Possibly as 9.
8\. & *Mate*. Lady holding flowers. As 9.
9\. & *Mate*. Lady holding flower. As 8.
9\. *Gardener*. Man with potted plant on plinth.
9\. *Lost Sheep Found*
10\. *Lost Piece*
19\. Reclining hind
20\. *O. Cromwell*
21\. *Bag Piper*
21\. Venus and Cupid
22\. Neptune
23\. St. George and the Dragon
28\. *King David*
29\. *King David*
30\. *Mower*
31\. Hay maker. As 33.
31\. *Hay Maker.* Different head to other examples.
33\. *Hay Maker.* As 31.
33\. Bull baiting
36\. *Game-keeper*
37\. *Van Tromp*. As 38.
38\. *Van Tromp*. As 37.
41\. Hudibras. As 42.
42\. Hudibras. As 41.
42\. *Dr. Franklin*. As 43.
43\. *Dr. Franklin*. As 42.
43\. *Apollo.* As 45.
44\. *Diana*

45. *Apollo*. As 43.
48. & *Lady*. Lady holding a bird.
49. Dutch Boy
50. Dutch Girl
52. Venus holding a bird
53. *Minerva*. As 59.
55. *Old Age*. Woman with crutches.
57. Venus holding a bird
59. *Minerva*. As 53.
62. Vicar and Moses (in pulpit)
63. *Vicar and Moses* (in pulpit)
65. *Gasconian*. As 66, 67, 68, 99.
66. *A Gasconian*. As 65, 67, 68, 99.
67. Girl with pitcher on head
67. *Gasconian*. As 65, 66, 68, 99.
68. *Gasconian*. As 65, 66, 67, 99.
68. *Peasant Worshiping*. As *Worshiper* 69, 70, hat placed differently.
69. *Spanish Shepherd*
69. *Worshiper*. As 68, hat placed differently, and 70.
70. *Worshiper*. As 69.
71. *Spinning*
71. *Spanish Dancer.* Male.
72. *Spanish Dancer.* Female.
73. *Spanish Dancer*. Female.
74. *Sweep Boy.* Probably as 5, 6.
78. *Jupiter.* Model with eagle to the left.[15]
79. *Jupiter.* Model with eagle to the left.
80. Bust of Handel
81. Bust of Milton. Probably as 82.
82. Bust of Milton. Larger than and different from 128. H: 10.3".
82. Bust of a divine
87. Girl feeding birds
88. Shepherd and shepherdess musicians
89. Couple with birdcage
89. Shepherd and shepherdess musician with candleholder
90. Couple with birdcage with candleholder
92. Bust of Zingara
96. Boy, arms folded. Possible Cymon, as 135.
96. Iphigenia. As 136.
99. Gasconian. Probably intended to read 66.
103. Hercules
112. Bust of Shakespeare
117. *St. Peter.* Also recorded titled *St. Petrus*
118. St. Peter. As 117.
119. *St. Phillip*
119. St John
120. *St. Paul*
121. St. Phillip. Probably as 119.
122. *St. Andrew*. As 152.
123. Bust of Voltaire
127. Small bust of Milton. Probably as 128.
128. Small bust of a Milton. Smaller than and different from 81, 82. H: 6.9".
131. *Scuffle*. As 134.
131. *Flemish Music.* Male. As 132 male.
131. *Flemish Music.* Female. As 132 female.
132. *Flemish Music.* Male. As 131 male.
132. *Flemish Music.* Female. As 131 female.
133. *Contest*
134. *Scuffle*
134. *Friendship*. As 154.
135. *Falconer*
135. Cymon
136. Iphigenia. As 96.
136. & *Partner.* Lady holding goose.
137. Chaucer
137. Newton
140. *Virgin Mary*
150. Goat with kid
152. *St. Andrew*. As 122.
153. *Tenderness*
154. *Friendship*. As 134.
155. Chaucer
163. Shepherd and shepherdess spill vase
164. Boy bird nesting spill vase
165. Boy and squirrel spill vase
166. *Rural Pastime*
169. Fortune. Lady with cornucopia.
169. *Elijah*
170. *Widow of Sarepta*

15. Other Makers' Marks

The following marks have been noted on enamel-painted figures and busts that, unless otherwise indicated, are shown in this work.

William Absolon: the mark "Absolon Yarm" is a painter's mark. William Absolon of Yarmouth (1751–1815) established a retail shop in Yarmouth in 1784, selling pottery, porcelain, and glass.[1] From around 1790, he bought items in the white from manufacturers throughout England, and he painted them.[2] He died in 1815. His mark is recorded beneath the bases of figures emblematic of autumn and water shown in this work, as well as figures of Venus,[3] Hope,[4] Neptune[5], and a girl vendor holding a basket and wearing a bonnet.[6]

Barker, Sutton, & Till: a transfer-printed mark, "B. S. & T." above "Burslem" amidst scrolls and foliage, is on at least two busts of W. Clowes of the same form. This partnership is recorded in *Pigot's Directory* of 1830, 1835, and 1841.

Bott & Co.: "Bott & Co" is recorded impressed on two busts of Shakespeare of the same form. Trade directories of 1809, 1811, and 1816 list Thomas Bott & Co. of Lane End.

Brameld: the impressed "BRAMELD" mark was used by John and William Brameld at the Swinton Pottery, Yorkshire, between 1806 and 1826. It is recorded only on a deer impressed "BRAMELD/5" and a pair of figures of Jobson and Nell, each impressed "BRAMELD+4".[7]

John Cartledge: a pair of candlesticks formed as Ceres and Diana is inscribed "John Cartledge at the Lodge in the plantation CROWBRIDGE 1800".[8]

Dixon, Austin, & Co.: the Sunderland Pottery, also known as the "Garrison" Pottery because of its proximity to the town's garrison, was in use from 1753 to 1865. In 1818, John Phillips withdrew from the partnership, and from December 1818, Robert Dixon, William Austin, and Thomas Henderson operated it as Dixon, Austin, & Co.[9] At some stage, Henderson left the partnership and Alexander Phillips joined, but the partnership continued as Dixon, Austin, & Co. until its dissolution on December 31, 1839.[10] Figures marked "DIXON, AUSTIN, & Co" can thus be dated to between December 1818 and 1839.

Dixon, Austin, & Co. produced an extensive range of wares, but only a few marked enamel-painted figures are recorded. These are known from figures of the Four Seasons (including a handful of complete sets) and from watch stands of two forms. All use the pink luster associated with the northeast pot banks, but Staffordshire pot banks used pink luster too.

Thomas Fell: "FELL" is impressed beneath a figure of Apollo. The mark is that of the Newcastle-upon-Tyne potter Thomas Fell (active from 1817), better known for his under-glaze colored wares. The impressed mark "FELL NEWCASTLE B" occurs beneath a watch stand with a small recumbent lion on its base.

John Forster: "Iohn Forster made this at Hanley Agust [sic] the 29 1820" is inscribed beneath an inkstand fashioned as a cherub astride a dolphin (Fitzwilliam Museum c.981–1911).

Thomas Greatbatch: "Thomas Greatbatch 1809" and "Captain Berry" are inscribed beneath a bust of Sir Edward Berry, (Volume 4, fig. 200.82).

Thomas Gruitt: a bust of the Empress Josephine is inscribed "Thomas Gruitt 1809" on the reverse.[11]

Thomas Hanshall: "Thomas Hanshall July 1 1821" is painted conspicuously on the front of an unusual bull baiting group. It seems unlikely that a painter would have the audacity to sign his work in this way, so the mark is assumed to be that of a small potter.

Herculaneum: "HERCULANEUM", the mark of the Herculaneum Pottery in Liverpool, is impressed on busts of Lord St. Vincent and Lord Duncan.

J. Jarvis: two busts of military or naval men are both impressed "J.JARVIS JANUARY 12TH 1826". Joseph Jarvis was a Staffordshire china and earthenware dealer based in Blyth Marsh, Staffordshire.[12]

Thomas Leek: a large figure of Venus de Medici is inscribed on the base "THOMAS LEEK 1819". The figure may be from the same molds as Volume 4, figure 194.43.[13]

Benjamin Plant: "Benjamin Plant Lane End" (the first name may be abbreviated to "B") is incised beneath several large lions. The lions sometimes occur decorated in silver luster, indicating they were made some time after 1804.

Milton: "MILTON" is impressed beneath the base of a small pug.

J. Morris, Stoke: The impressed mark "J. MORRIS STOKE" occurs beneath bear baiting jugs with detachable heads that date from the 1825–1835 period.

Turner: "TURNER" is impressed in very small letters beneath a figural spill vase. Trade directories of 1781, 1783, and 1784 record John Turner of Lane End, who died in 1787. His sons, William and John, also of Lane End, are recorded in directories of 1796 and 1802. By 1806, the brothers were bankrupt. William operated a small manufactory from 1807 to 1812 and again from 1824 to 1829, and his brother John potted for a brief period in 1814.[14]

Selman: "SELMAN" is impressed on the reverse of a sheep with bocage. The Selman name is associated with J. & W. Selman, toy makers, circa 1860, but the sheep is, to all appearances, pre-Victorian.

Pierre Stephan: "Stephan F" is incised on a figure of either the Duke of York or the Duke of Clarence and on a figure of the Duke of Wellington. This is the mark of the Derby modeler Pierre Stephan, who free-lanced from about 1773 until 1798. The same mark is incised on the reverse of a bust of Nelson, impressed *"NELSON"* on the front of the plinth (Royal Greenwich Museums, AAA6023).

Peter Vanina: the letters "P.V." impressed into large classical figures are the initials of the London plaster maker, Peter Vanina. The initials were impressed into the plaster from which the figure was molded.

16. Blue Group
(circa 1820–1830)

The Blue Group is so dubbed because most of its figures have cobalt blue bases with large areas left in the white. These striking bases alone do not equate with an attribution to the Group, and some Blue Group examples exhibit almost no blue enameling.

Bocage flowers, more so than leaves, are helpful in confirming a Blue Group attribution. The following leaf and flower forms occur on Blue Group examples (fig. 16.2).

1. Five-leaflet frond with three flowers integral to the frond. The frond itself is rather generic in appearance. However, two of the flowers are unusual and have five petals, while the third flower is a modified carnation with a particularly proud center. This combination of leaves and flowers appears to be specific to the Blue Group. The presence of these flowers on bases is also a useful indicator of attribution to this Group because flowers of this very form have not yet been observed on figures attributable to any other Group.
2. Fern frond with specific flowers. Fern fronds usually comprise seven tiny fern leaflets. On occasion, these are not particularly well defined and may have five leaflets. As fern fronds are common, the flowers are critical to attribution. The distinctive five-petalled flowers described previously, sometimes together with a star-shaped flower, occur on those fern fronds that link to the Blue Group. Frequently, small star-shaped flowers (or clusters of these flowers) are on the fronds, and in these instances other factors must support attribution.
3. Broad frond. This frond has four sections (possibly leaflets) and is v-shaped at the top. In one instance of a figure attributed to this Group, atypical four-petalled flowers were on three fronds.
4. Modified seven-leaflet fern frond. The addition of two tiny leaflets and two stubby flower stalks to the midline of the frond results in a form that is specific to this Group.

Figure 16.1. The New Marriage Act, *WATER*. Attributed to Blue Group. H: ~7" max.

Figure 16.2. The reverse of two Blue Group figures showing unpainted surfaces.

Figure 16.3. Blue Group bocage fronds and flowers. *1*. Five-leaflet frond with specific flowers. *2*. Fern-leaflet fronds with specific flowers. *3*. Broad frond, v-shaped at the top. *4*. Modified seven-leaflet fern frond.

Blue Group fronds can be painted very distinctively. The fronds may be edged or partially edged in blue. Sometimes the edging is blue, but half of each frond front is painted green and half is unpainted. Such fronds are usually unpainted at the back, and much of the reverse of the figure, including the bocage, tree trunk, and base, may be unpainted. This mode of decoration is only found on figures that can be attributed to the Blue Group (fig. 16.3).

17. Box Title Group
(circa 1825–1835)

Figure 17.1. *VILLAGE GROUP, SAMUEL ANOINTING DAVID.* Attributed to Box Title Group. H: 7.3" (L), 7.1" (R).

The Box Title Group is so named because titles on its figures are outlined by a box-like frame. Not all figures titled in this manner are attributable to the Box Title Group, and not all Box Title Group examples are titled! In fact, many features on Box Title figures are not specific to the Group, but in combination these features only occur on Box Title examples. Because some of the figure forms within the Box Title Group are specific to the Group, all Box Title examples are thought to have originated from the same pot bank. In addition, subtle details, such as the appearance of glazes and enamels, reinforce the conviction that these figures form a cohesive cluster.

Box Title bocages are thickly potted. They only use the common five-leaflet fronds used by many pot banks, but the fronds are seldom dense. Rather, the bocage tree often appears spindly, with bare branches exposed (fig. 17.1).

Box Title bocage flowers are always carnations, like those that many pot banks used. These carnations are usually thickly potted, are on fat stalks, and are painted as seen in figure 17.2. The most distinctive style has only the petal centers and flower centers painted, leaving the petals outlined in white. Carnations painted in this eye-catching manner usually suggest a Box Title attribution.

Figure 17.2. Box Title carnations are painted as shown here, but colors may vary.

Many Box Title figures are titled. The title is always impressed into the clay within an impressed frame. Both the title and the frame are painted dark brown or black. Scrolling on bases, when present, may be yellow or blue. A two-tone palette in green and turquoise is sometimes used on bases. This pleasingly pretty combination appears to be specific to the Group (fig. 17.3).

Figure 17.3. *SHEPERDISS;* a pointer. Attributed to Box Title Group. Both figures have typical two-tone bases. H: 5.5" (L), 5" (R). *Right: Peter Flemans.*

18. Brown Base Group
(circa 1800)

Figure 18.1. Neptune, Venus. Attributed to Brown Base Group. H: 8.5" (L), 9.2" (R).

The Brown Base Group is named for a small but clear-cut group of classical figures easily identified by the characteristics of their bases. The bases are rectangular and painted brown, and each internal corner has been made angular by what appears to be a single knife cut (fig. 18.2). This slashing of the internal corners of bases is an unusual feature that occurs on nearly every example.[1] It also occurs on some Neale figures and on many Lakin & Poole figures. However, Neale figures are markedly different in style and decoration. Lakin & Poole figures can be stylistically similar, but their enamels are less dense, and their bases are usually painted with delicate marbling and often bear titles.

Figure 18.2. The interior of a Brown Base Group base, showing cut internal corners.

The Brown Base Group comprises classical figure subjects only. Typically the figures are decorated with robust enamel colors, some of which may have been sponged to soften them. The figures have a common appearance that makes them easily recognizable. However, the following figures may or may not belong to this Group (fig. 18.3).

> A figure of Ceres from the same molds as Brown Base examples and with a base that has cut internal corners has a vermicular pattern painted on its base. Perhaps the Brown Base manufactory occasionally painted its wares in a different palette.
>
> A figure of Minerva from the same molds as the Brown Base figure occurs on a marbled base. Both bases have cut internal corners, but the figure on a marbled base is painted with more delicate enamels. Perhaps the Brown Base manufactory made this figure. On the other hand, the subtle enamels raise the possibility that Lakin & Poole made it. Brown Base figures appear to postdate Lakin figures, and perhaps the Lakin molds passed to the Brown Base manufactory.

Figure 18.3. Ceres on a brown base and on a vermicular base, both from the same molds; Minerva on a brown base and a marbled base, both from the same molds. Possibly the Brown Base manufactory made all four figures.

Interestingly, marked Dale figures of Aesculapius and Mercury use the same figure molds as Brown Base examples (Volume 4, chapters 156, 184). These are very rare figures. That only Dale and Brown Base made figures of Mercury and Aesculapius suggests an association between Dale and Brown Base. Brown Base figures, with their square bases and lack of bocages, appear to be typical of the early 1800s, whereas Dale figures, usually with bocages and brighter enamels, seem to be more typical of the 1820s. Perhaps Dale acquired Brown Base molds when that pot bank ceased operations.

19. Leather Leaf Group
(circa 1820–1830)

The Leather Leaf Group is named for the appearance of the bocage leaves on many of its figures. Some bocage leaves curl in the manner of a stiff, overly dry piece of leather. Curled leaves occasionally occur on figures attributable to other Groups, but fortunately the Leather Leaf Group is rich in additional features that can confirm attribution.

Figure 19.1. Setter, mower holding a scythe, cow. Attributed to Leather Leaf Group. H: 7.4" max.

Most Leather Leaf bocage leaves are flat, but frequently a prominent leaf or two in the bocage is curled. Each curled leaf is one-sided (i.e., the leaf does not consist of two clay components placed back-to-back). The following leaf forms occur on Leather Leaf bocages (fig. 19.2).

1. Fern frond. Each frond comprises either five or seven tiny fern leaflets. These fronds are not unlike those used by other pot banks, and, although Leather Leaf examples are somewhat differently potted, it is uncertain whether the subtle differences result in a leaf form that is peculiar to this Group.
2. Hawthorn leaf frond. Each frond comprises three hawthorn leaves, much like similar fronds by other potters.
3. Elongated oak leaf. This leaf form is specific to the Group.
4. Leaflets arranged in threes. A splayed frond of generic leaflets in threes. These fronds have only been observed without curled leaves.

Figure 19.2. Leather Leaf Group bocage leaves and fronds: *1*. Fern fronds. *3*. Elongated oak leaf. Leaf forms not shown here are described within the text.

Figure 19.3. Flowers and acorns specific to the Leather Leaf Group: *1.* Five-petalled flower. *2.* Four-petalled flower. *3.* Starfish flower. This is the largest flower. *4.* Acorns with an acorn cup.

Leather Leaf Group flowers are routinely found on both the bocages and bases of figures and include the small six-petalled flowers and large cabbage roses used by several pot banks. However, the following flowers are specific to this Group and can be particularly helpful in establishing an attribution (fig. 19.3).

1. Five-petalled flower. A round flower with five scallops for petals and a well-defined center occurs frequently. Crisply potted examples of this flower show exquisite attention to detail in the mold. Each flower is painted either red or blue around its edge, and the center, if painted, is yellow. This leaves an unpainted white area in the middle of the flower.
2. Four-petalled flower. This flower is like the previous flower, but it has only four petals.
3. Starfish flower. A flower with five long petals radiating from a central disk has only been recorded on bases, as it is too large for bocages. Typically, such flowers are painted in the same manner as the round flowers.
4. Acorns. These are usually arranged in clusters. Sometimes an empty acorn cup is included.

Figure 19.4. Detail of a Leather Leaf Group base decorated with the long leaves specific to the Group.

Leather Leaf bases are very helpful in establishing an attribution. This manufactory took unusual care in decorating bocage trunks and bases, and some of the most eye-catching bases are associated with this Group. Flowers specific to the Leather Leaf Group are frequently strewn on bases, along with the odd bocage leaf or two. A very long, narrow leaf (often over 1.5") is sometimes applied atop the base. It is usually painted a soft turquoise, and its gently serrated edges make it appear to have been cut from leather with a pair of scissors. This leaf is specific to the Leather Leaf Group (fig. 19.4).

Figure 19.5. Leather Leaf Group bases showing typical formation and decoration.

Leather Leaf Group figures can be painted in a recognizable style. Bases are frequently enameled in splotchy greens and browns. Yellow is sometimes dabbed on too, and that same color tends to be used for the interiors of spills. When blue scrolling is present, the scrolls are painted with heavy brush strokes. Some figures have a geometrically-shaped base banded with a raised frieze that is integral to the base. The frieze may be a repeating *fleur-de-lis* or leaf-type design, and the design is usually picked out in colors. Several variations have been noted, and in all instances multiple features have supported a Leather Leaf attribution. Bases of this type, thus, appear to be specific to the Leather Leaf Group (fig. 19.5).

20. Patriotic Group
(active circa 1810–1830)

In 1991, figure groups described as having "bases with S and C-scrolls where the white body is enhanced with red and blue enamels" were loosely described as belonging to the Patriotic Group.[1] That name has stuck to this Group. On the whole, figures with these scrolled bases are rich in detail, and systematic classification has identified a sizable number of related figures. Some of the figures have the red, white, and blue base scrolls that give the Patriotic Group its name, but many do not. The figures tend to be rather refined, and some of the finest figures of the period are attributable to the Patriotic Group.

Figure 20.1. Musical trio, with bocage. Attributed to Patriotic Group. H: 8.1".

Figure 20.2. Patriotic Group bocage leaf and frond forms: *1*. Five-leaflet frond. *2*. One leaflet atop five others. *3*. Three hawthorn leaves in a frond. *4*. Holly leaf. *5*. Cilantro frond. *6*. Pinecone frond. *7*. Three-leaflet frond. *8*. Seven-leaflet fern frond. *9*. Six-leaflet frond. *10*. Anthemion-type frond. *11*. Other leaf forms.

The Patriotic Group uses the following eleven leaf forms for bocages (fi 20.2).

1. Five-leaflet frond. Many pot banks used this frond form. Although subtle nuances differentiate Patriotic Group fronds (they can be particularly crisply defined and a little on the short side), the fronds cannot be used to substantiate an attribution. However, they usually occur in conjunction with the distinctive Patriotic Group flowers discussed below.

2. One leaflet atop five others. Fronds of this form are not exclusive to the Patriotic Group, but in nearly all instances, they are on figures with other features linking them to the Group.

3. Three hawthorn leaves in a frond. Other pot banks made similar fronds. Patriotic Group examples can occur with or without flowers.

4. Holly leaf. The holly leaf is large, and berries are integral to the front and back of the leaf. The berries are picked out in color on the fronts of the leaves, as shown in figure 20.2, but not on the backs. Sometimes the leaves are arranged quite creatively (perhaps one pointing up and the other down), and on tithe pig figure groups the leaves curl forward for a cascading effect. In all but a few instances, holly leaves occur on figures that exhibit other Patriotic Group characteristics, and the holly leaf is thought to be exclusive to the Patriotic Group.

5. Cilantro frond. Three curly cilantro leaves are arranged in a frond. Such fronds are not specific to the Patriotic Group. In the example shown in figure 20.2, the flower stalks have been painted to simulate flowers.

6. Pinecone frond. Each frond comprises eight little pinecones. Fronds of this form are specific to the Patriotic Group, and they never have flowers on them.

7. Three-leaflet frond. This small frond form is only recorded on bocages arranged in an arc. Two variations have been noted. In one, the leaflets are finer and have pointed tips. In the other, the leaflets are stubbier, with rounded tips.

8. Seven-leaflet fern frond. This frond is not unlike the fern fronds used by other potters, but it is tooled somewhat differently and has a prominent central vein. It occurs only occasionally.

9. Six-leaflet frond. Small figures with side bocages often have a six-leaflet frond to either side. At first glance, each frond appears to consist of two three-leaf fronds, but the six leaves were in fact molded as one. These fronds are not exclusive to the Group.

10. Anthemion-type frond. Other potters also used this frond, which occurs only occasionally on Patriotic Group examples.

11. Other leaf forms. On rare occasions, other leaf forms have been noted on figures that are confidently attributable to the Patriotic Group. Three such forms are shown in figure 20.2. These leaves do not link to any other pot bank and, as the Patriotic Group is so very large, variations such as these are not too surprising.

Figure 20.3. Flowers and sprigs exclusive to the Patriotic Group. The Patriotic flower is shown on the left, with variations in painting. On the right are two sprigs characteristic of the Group.

Patriotic Group bocages often have small flowers with six or eight petals, and sometimes large cabbage roses occur, particularly on bases. These flowers are not exclusive to the Group. Importantly, the Patriotic Group is associated with a very specific flower, dubbed the "Patriotic flower." This largish flower measures ½" to ¾" in diameter and is almost always painted with either red or blue petals. Its presence alone almost validates an attribution. Figure 20.3 shows two examples of the flower, and the flower is also evident on the bocage in figure 20.1. At quick glance, the Patriotic flower resembles the Tunstall flower. However, the Patriotic flower is larger, the petals are "toothier," and the center is demarcated differently.

Two floral sprigs are exclusive to the Patriotic Group. These usually occur on bases and are very helpful in attributing figures. The more common sprig comprises three small flowers set among pointed leaves. Less commonly, two flowers and a bunch of grapes are set among pointed leaves (fig. 20.3). Also, sprigs fashioned from one or other of the Patriotic Group leaves are quite common. These sprigs usually comprise a leaf or leaves anchored by a single flower.

The Patriotic Group produced a very broad range of figures on multiple bases, only a few of which are shown in figure 20.4. With the exception of the third and fourth examples, all the bases are probably specific to the Group. When titled, titling is sometimes done in a manner that is exclusive to the Group. The title may be impressed on a small tablet of clay that is applied separately to the base. The shape of the tablet varies, and it is unpainted or painted yellow.

Patriotic Group figures are, on the whole, particularly finely modeled, and the overall quality of the painting and glazes is superior. Dress patterns can be quite detailed, with fine floral or lace-like patterns painted in iron red. Because the subject range is so broad, figures from the same molds occur repeatedly in different contexts, and bases of the same form are found on dissimilar figures and groups. A broad date range of circa 1810 to 1830 seems appropriate for this Group.

Figure 20.4. Patriotic Group figures on typical bases. Titling on little clay tablets is a feature specific to the Group.

21. "Sherratt" Group
(circa 1820–1840)

Figure 21.1. Royal supporters spill vase with sheep. Attributed to "Sherratt." H: 8.8".

Obadiah Sherratt was an early nineteenth-century Burslem figure maker, but, because there are no known marked Sherratt figures, attribution to Sherratt is impossible. Nonetheless, over the years more figures have been attributed to Obadiah Sherratt than to any other potter. These attributions are baseless. The Sherratt myth began in the 1920s with the unsubstantiated attribution of bull baiting groups to Sherratt. The name Obadiah Sherratt rolls off the tongue rather dramatically, and over the decades the story acquired a life of its own. Increasingly, authoritative sources attributed to Sherratt figures in the style of vigorous bull baiting groups, along with a host of others. In recent years, a systematic study has convincingly linked specific figures to the so-called "Sherratt" bull baitings.[1] There is no denying the relationships between these figures, and they do need to be called something, so for convenience they are dubbed "Sherratt"—but they might as correctly be called by any other name. Figures in the "Sherratt" Group are feature-rich and together form the largest Group of figures. They have been fully explored elsewhere.[2]

For completeness, it is noted that Obadiah Sherratt was a Burslem figure potter of some significance. He was the son of a potter, William Sherratt. *Allbut's Directory* of 1822–1823 lists "Sherratt Obadiah, toy and figure maker, Hot Lane".[3] *Pigot's Directory* of 1828 lists "Skerratt Obad" as an earthenware manufacturer at Hot Lane, Burslem, and *Pigot's Directory* of 1830 lists Sherratt similarly, but now at Waterloo Road, Burslem. *White's Directory* of 1834 lists "Sharratt" as an "earthenware toy manufacturer" at the same location, and *Pigot's Directory* of 1841 records "Sherratt Obadiah" as a "Toy & Ornamental China Manufacturer" at Waterloo Road. Sherratt's will, executed in October 1842, is signed in his own hand. His considerable estate included multiple "Dwelling Houses" and "manufactory buildings and premises." The pot bank passed into the hands of his son, Hamlet, and that ownership is reflected in *Williams Directory* of 1846.

Seven leaf forms occur on "Sherratt" bocages. Six of these are shown in figure 21.2.

1. Three oak leaves in a frond. These fronds almost always occur in conjunction with one or other of the typical "Sherratt" flowers. Usually, the flowers are the four-petalled flowers dubbed "mayflowers."[4] Typically, three mayflowers are on each frond, placed either in a cluster or separately on each of the leaves, but sometimes a lone mayflower serves duty on a frond. This combination of triple-oak-leaf fronds and mayflowers is quite specific to "Sherratt." Several pot banks used triple-oak-leaf fronds, but "Sherratt" fronds are potted quite distinctively and never have the acorns that others favored.
2. One leaflet atop four others. Other potters used arrangements of one leaflet atop four, but "Sherratt" fronds differ in the detailing and are distinctive. This frond is encountered most often on small figures.
3. Five-leaflet fern frond. On rare occasions, these fronds are arranged in an arc, and sometimes three fronds are joined into a mega-frond. Other pot banks used similar fern fronds, but "Sherratt" fronds occur with one or other of the "Sherratt" flowers.
4. Five-leaflet frond. Very many potters used this generic frond, so other features are critical for attribution.
5. Double anthemion frond. Two swirled anthemion-shaped leaves combine in a frond. Again, the flower, rather than the frond, is helpful for attribution.
6. Two small oak leaflets atop three others. This frond occurs painted turquoise (on figures painted in a turquoise palette), but it is sometimes painted green. It is thought to be specific to "Sherratt."
7. Three hawthorn leaves in a frond. This frond occurs only rarely on "Sherratt" figures and is not illustrated here.

Figure 21.2. "Sherratt" bocage frond forms: *1.* Three oak leaves in each frond. *2.* One leaflet atop four others. *3.* Five-leaflet fern frond. *4.* Five-leaflet frond. *5.* Double anthemion frond. *6.* Two oak leaflets atop three.

Figure 21.3. Flowers on "Sherratt" bocages.

"Sherratt" bocage flowers are easily recognizable. They are well modeled and are often painted in one of three colors (blue, orange, and pink). Although other potters used most of these flower forms, the way in which "Sherratt" versions are tooled, coupled with their painting, makes them easily differentiable and quite eye-catching.

The eight flower forms recorded on "Sherratt" bocages are shown in figure 21.3. These flowers are most frequently seen on "Sherratt" figures. Flower 1, the so-called "mayflower," is the most common. Flower 6 is the largest of the flowers, and flower 8 is the tiniest. Flower 7 comprises a cluster of three little flowers (each with five cleft petals) formed as one in a single mold.

The most helpful "Sherratt" identifier is the floral sprig shown on the left of figure 21.4. This sprig is only found applied to "Sherratt" figures. It is akin to a signature. It is not integral to any other molded part but is formed separately in its own mold and then applied to the figure.

The teeny flowers shown on the right of figure 21.4 are strongly indicative of a "Sherratt" attribution. They are not found on bocages. Instead, they decorate anything from bonnet tops to flower pots. Because they are so minute, several usually occur together. Despite their size, each has a well-defined center, and one must marvel at the care needed to fashion them.

Figure 21.4. *Left:* the floral sprig that is only applied to "Sherratt" figures and alone substantiates an attribution. *Right:* the tiny decorative flowers that appear to be specific to "Sherratt."

The "Sherratt" Group is large and varied. The figures are particularly engaging and exude a naive and earthy charm. They are jam-packed with minutiae that draw the eye. Dress patterns on larger figures are detailed and usually have big, freely formed flowers and leaves against a white (unpainted) background broken by a pattern of large and small dots. "Sherratt" ladies frequently wear three-plumed cockades atop their heads. Touches of luster decoration are not uncommon. Significantly, most "Sherratt" bases are specific to their pot bank. Very many of them can be seen throughout this work. A sampling is shown in figure 21.5.

Generally, "Sherratt" examples appear to date from around 1820 or perhaps a little earlier, and the subject matter of some of the table-base figure groups dates them from 1834.

Figure 21.5. "Sherratt" figures stand on recognizable bases. Their decoration as much as their form makes them specific to "Sherratt."

22. Tunstall Group
(circa 1825–1835)

Figure 22.1. Gentleman bagpiper and lady with lute, a pair. Attributed to Tunstall Group. H: 7.1".

Figure 22.2. The Tunstall Group flower with a matching shard from the Tunstall site. This flower occurs only on Tunstall Group figures.

Excavations of the Tunstall site yielded bocage fragments bearing a very distinctive seven-petal flower, dubbed the "Tunstall flower." A shard with that flower is shown in figure 22.2 alongside a similar flower from a figure. Flowers of this form appear to be specific to the Tunstall Group and have enabled the identification of a substantial number of figures that share other common features.[6] Nearly every figure attributed to the Tunstall Group uses these Tunstall flowers, but in the odd instance, carnations occur instead, and a Tunstall shard does indeed sport a carnation. Because many potters used carnations, figures with carnations can only be attributed to the Tunstall Group if they exhibit other Tunstall features.

Most of the shards excavated at Tunstall show five-leaflet bocage fronds of the type so widely used by other potters as to be of no help in attributing figures. However, four distinctive five-leaflet frond forms appear to be particular to the Tunstall Group (figs. 22.3–22.6) Two of these frond forms occur among the shards, while a further two can be linked to the Tunstall Group through features on figures with these fronds. At the same time, caution is warranted, and the presence of any one of the four frond forms shown here cannot alone substantiate an attribution.

The 1972 excavation of a former Woolworth's store in High Street, Tunstall, revealed shards and fragments of earthenware figures that suggested the presence of a pot bank near that location.[1] Some of those shards have enabled attribution of extant figures to that manufactory. Because the Tunstall shards link to many figures that seem to postdate 1820, their potter must have been active for some years from the 1820s. Clearly, these discoveries invite the detection of the manufacturer that produced the so-called Tunstall figures. The following specialist figure makers fit the bill:

> George Hood was born in 1780 and is first recorded in *Pigot's Directory* of 1822 as potting toys only in Tunstall. In 1831, Hood bought land and built the Highgate Pottery in Tunstall,[2] which he operated until his bankruptcy in around 1839. Hood died in 1848.[3]
>
> Michael Tunnicliffe is not noted in 1822 directories, but he is listed in 1828 and 1830 directories as a manufacturer of only toys or figures in Tunstall. Specifically, *White's Directory* of 1834 records Tunnicliffe as a manufacturer of both china and earthenware figures on High Street.[4] He is last listed in *Pigot's Directory* of 1841 as having premises at both Tunstall and Longton.
>
> Samuel Grocott, like Tunnicliffe, is not recorded in 1822 directories. He debuts in *Pigot's Directory* of 1828 as a toy manufacturer at Liverpool Road, Tunstall. Apparently, this enterprise was short-lived, for the next year Grocott advertised in the *Staffordshire Advertiser* to let his small earthenware manufactory and adjoining malt kiln in the center of Tunstall, along with a steam mill nearby.[5] Perhaps Samuel Grocott then partnered with Daniel Edge in neighboring Burslem to produce figures marked "EDGE & GROCOTT".

Despite their different addresses, the Hood, Tunnicliffe, and Grocott manufactories were in close proximity to today's High Street. Any one of these manufactories might have dumped shards on a High Street waste site; or possibly the earth holding the shards shifted to High Street over time. Notably, the Tunstall manufactory produced more than one model of several of its subjects, suggesting that the pot bank operated for a number of years and updated its models periodically. This would eliminate Samuel Grocott as the manufacturer in question. While it is possible that one of Tunstall's several general earthenware manufactories also potted figures as a sideline, it seems that either George Hood or Michael Tunnicliffe was the manufacturer of the figures loosely dubbed "Tunstall."

1. Small five-leaflet frond. This stubby derivative of the generic five-leaflet frond appears to be exclusive to Tunstall. It occurs on both extant figures and as an excavated shard (fig. 22.3).

Figure 22.3. The Tunstall Group's small five-leaflet frond. The frond is shown with a matching Tunstall shard and a sheep with a bocage comprising these fronds.

2. Elongated, sharply splayed five-leaflet frond. The ends of these long leaves are blunt, and the first and last leaves are arranged in a straight line. This structure is exclusive to the Tunstall Group and matches excavated shards (fig. 22.4).

Figure 22.4. The Tunstall Group's elongated, sharply splayed five-leaflet frond. The frond is shown with a matching Tunstall shard and a deer with a bocage comprising these fronds.

3. Large five-leaflet frond with pointed leaves. This frond has hitherto only been recorded on figures that have other Tunstall Group attributes (fig. 22.5).

Figure 22.5. The Tunstall Group's large five-leaflet frond with pointed tips. The front and the back of a frond are shown, as is a musician with a bocage comprising these fronds.

4. Small five-leaflet frond with pointed leaf tips. This frond is smaller and simpler than the previous frond and occurs only on figures that have other features linking them to Tunstall (fig. 22.6).

Figure 22.6. The Tunstall Group's small five-leaflet frond with pointed tips. The front and the back of a frond are shown, as is a deer with a bocage comprising these fronds.

Tunstall figures are sometimes titled. In these cases, the letters are always impressed into the figure. The title is usually, but not always, placed in a yellow-painted reserve area on the front of the base. One of the Tunstall shards shows a white (glazed only) bocage leaf with just the edges painted blue. Several Tunstall Group figures with similarly painted leaves have been identified, as have some with comparable green and white leaves. Other figures attributable to the Tunstall Group have the backs of their bocages unpainted (fig. 22.7). These features are helpful in confirming an attribution, but other pot banks occasionally decorated their bocages similarly.

Figure 22.7. A couple drinking beer, *VILLAGE GROUP*. Both are attributed to Tunstall Group. L: 8.7", R: 7.5". Note the peculiarly painted bocage leaves and a title impressed within a yellow-painted area. The reverse of the left-hand group is unpainted. *Left: Brighton and Hove Museums.*

23. Other Groups

Several small groupings of figures form well demarcated clusters. These Groups seem to be the work of small pot banks, rather than subsets of the output of more prolific manufactories. Future discoveries may reveal additional features that will determine the status of each of these small Groups.

Figure 23.1. Shepherd musician. Attributed to Big Blossom Group. H: 5". Alongside is the flower that gives this Group its name.

1. **The Big Blossom Group** (fig. 23.1) is named for the truly enormous blossoms on its bocages. Several pot banks used assorted large flowers, but Big Blossom flowers are particularly large and of a specific form. Each flower measures about 1" across and has seven petals that present as a frill. The center is well-defined, with a tiny impressed design visible on sharply potted examples. Typically, the edges of petals and the centers of flowers are painted an often-bright color, with much of each petal left unpainted. The result is eye-catching. Bocages on recorded examples are all fashioned in the same way and all use leaflets much like those used for generic five-leaflet fronds. The leaflets are arranged symmetrically in a fan-like shape to form a frond. Then, an additional leaflet is placed atop. Examples with five, seven, and nine leaflets defining the frond have been recorded hitherto. Other potters fashioned similar fronds, but Big Blossom fronds are especially thinly potted and rather ill-defined.

Figure 23.2. Gentleman gardener, lady gardener. Attributed to Gray Base Group. H: 6.2" each.

2. **The Gray Base Group** (fig. 23.2) is named for the gray color of most figures' bases. All bases are square and most are painted gray, but the base is almost yellow on occasion. Also, two figures on black bases have been linked to this Group because of their close similarity to figures on gray bases. Thirteen figure forms, all rather like figures made by sundry other potters, have been identified. The figures are consistently well glazed with bright, hard glazes, and they are carefully painted. Bocages, when present, have non-specific anthemion leaves.

3. **The Daisy Group** (fig. 23.3) is named for its distinctive daisy-like bocage flowers. The figures generally resemble marked Salt figures. Bocages always use common five-leaflet fronds. Flowers have six floppy petals and are applied directly to the bocage fronds (without stalks). A tooled tree joint on the bocage trunk is apparently specific to the Daisy Group. In joining the upper bocage tree-trunk to the lower part (the latter is part of the base mold), the potter used a tool that left a transverse groove. This joint can be very untidy. Not all figures with daisies show this joint. Sometimes, a figure with a tooled tree joint has carnations rather than daisies, but in such instances close resemblances to figures with daisies support the belief that the tooled joint is exclusive to the Daisy Group.[1] Seven pairs of small figures have been identified (pairs of cows, deer, sheep, gardeners, shepherd and shepherdess, show man and show woman, and a boy with a dog to pair with a girl with a lamb), as well as a small lion.

Figure 23.3. *GIRL AND LAMB*. Attributed to Daisy Group. H: ~5.8". Alongside are details of the characteristic bocage flower and the tooled tree joint sometimes found on figures from this Group.

4. The Straw Flower Group (fig. 23.4) is named for the floral design integral to each base. The design varies but it consistently incorporates straw flowers with rather spiky petals. Picked out in colors against the green base, they are striking. Bocages use the common five-leaflet frond. Flowers are not specific to the Group. Most commonly, a tiny five-petalled flower with a cleft in the center of each petal is seen, but other flowers occur too. The figures tend to be less refined and on the lines of Salt-type figures. Examples include the run-of-the-mill gardeners, shepherds, and other small animal models, but a few models may be specific to this Group, such as the cow shown in figure 23.4

Figure 23.4. Cow. Attributed to Straw Flower Group. H: 6.3". *www.madelena.com.*

5. The Leaf Mat Group (fig. 23.5) is named for its bocages. Bocages usually comprise a single large frond, or sometimes two large fronds. Each frond resembles a mat assembled by carefully placing small leaves to cover a round area, with all the leaves funneling downward. The result is a large, rounded frond of many tightly-packed leaflets. Although each frond comprises many leaflets, the frond is made from just two molds (one for the front and one for the back). Little round flower stalks, used as attachment points for flowers, are among the leaflets and seem to be integral to the frond mold. In most cases, the entire frond is painted green and no flowers are added. Sometimes, the flower stalks are dabbed with paint to simulate flowers, and sometimes flowers are actually placed atop the stalks. Flowers range from the mundane to the unusual, and in some instances, large clusters of four flowers (molded as one) decorate the bocage. Most Leaf Mat figures are small subjects (animals in particular), but the pot bank did venture further, as evidenced by a New Marriage Act and performing animal troupe.

Figure 23.5. Spill vase with sheep and lamb. Attributed to Leaf Mat Group. H: 4.4". Detail of the reverse of the bocage is alongside.

6. The Grape Group (fig. 23.6) is named for the bunches of grapes placed on bocages in lieu of flowers. The grapes are painted purple. Leaves are compound fern-leaflets and are quite thickly potted, but it is the grapes on the bocages that make figures in this Group distinctive. A tithe pig group and small figures on square bases are recorded with these bocages.

Figure 23.6. Tithe pig. Attributed to Grape Group. H: 8.3". Detail of the bocage is alongside.

Figure 23.7. Deer. Attributed to Starred Anthemion Group. H: ~6".

7. The Starred Anthemion Group (fig. 23.7) is named for its distinctive combination of bocage leaves and flowers. The bocage leaves are anthemion-shaped, and the four-petalled flowers (frequently blue, sometimes pink) stand out like stars. All recorded figures are animal subjects.

Pastimes

24. Gardening

By the late eighteenth century, the love of gardening had crossed all social divides, and Staffordshire's figure potters were producing a plethora of gardening figures to adorn the homes of gardening enthusiasts. Today, figures of gardeners attest to the ongoing popularity of that theme throughout the pre-Victorian era. In particular, small gardener figures with bocages are common, but a pair in good condition can be elusive.

Figure 24.1. Tree grafter, with bocage. H: 8.6". The companion figure follows. The pair is rare. Price C, pair.

Figure 24.2. Tree grafter's companion, with bocage. H: 8.5". Pairs with the previous figure. Price C, pair.

Figure 24.3. Tree grafter and companion, reverse of previous pair. The dazzling bocages are unrestored. More commonly, these figures occur with major bocage losses.

Ralph Wood made the earliest attributable gardening figures (pages 75–79). Impressed numbers on some Ralph Wood figures seem to indicate a sequential introduction of models, and, for this reason, the small Ralph Wood male gardener and his companion, impressed "1" and "2", are thought to have been introduced in the 1780s (fig. 24.104). These figures inspired similarly styled figures of gardeners in ensuing decades.

Ralph Wood's small gardener figures must have been commercially successful because he made a second slightly larger pair. The bigger figures, usually titled *Gardener* and *& Mate,* occur impressed "8" and "9", and their low numbers in the 170-number range again indicate a relatively early production date in the Wood period (fig. 24.110). These gardener figures are also found with bocages and decorated in a manner suggestive of later Wood production, and, in these instances, their hats may be modified (figs. 24.115–120). All Ralph Wood figures predate 1802, but their form was mimicked by other potters in later years.

The lady companion to Ralph Wood's gardener holds a flower rather than the watering can that most other lady gardeners hold. Possibly this figure form inspired the host of small figures holding flowers.

Figure 24.4. Tree grafter, with bocage. H: 6.6". Most of the bocage is lost. Probably from the same pot bank as the previous tree grafter. These three-leaflet bocage fronds are found on an unclassified group of fine figures. Price A.

Figure 24.5. Tree grafter, with bocage. Attributed to Patriotic Group. H: ~7"*. Much of the bocage is lost, but the distinctive flowers confirm the attribution. Price A. * ~ = approximately. *Andrew Dando Antiques.*

Figure 24.6. Tree grafter, reverse of previous figure. This figure originally had a less ambitious bocage than the first tree grafter shown. *Andrew Dando Antiques.*

Figure 24.7. Tree grafter's companion, with bocage. Attributed to Patriotic Group. H: 7.5". The sprig atop the flower pot is characteristic of the Group. The fine pattern on her skirt and the red and blue scrolling are also typical features. Bocage restored. Price A.

Figure 24.8. Lady and gentleman gardeners, a pair, with bocages. Attributed to Leather Leaf Group. H: 9.3". A rare pair and attractive, despite the losses. The flowers on the bases are specific to the Group. Price B. *Andrew Dando Antiques.*

Figure 24.9. Gentleman gardener. Possibly attributable to Leather Leaf Group. H: 10". The similarity to the previous male figure suggests the attribution, but several pot banks used this bocage. Price A. *Andrew Dando Antiques.*

Figure 24.10. Gentleman gardener. H: 9.4". Made without bocage. Price B. *Image courtesy of The Potteries Museum & Art Gallery, Stoke-on-Trent, UK.*

Figure 24.11. Gentleman gardener and companion, a pair. H: 9.4". Made without bocages. The gardener's spade is restored. Price B. *Elinor Penna.*

Figure 24.12. Gentleman and lady gardeners, with bocage. H: 7.5". Like the following two groups, in the style of Walton. Cannot be attributed to Walton because a marked Walton example has not been recorded. Price B.

Figure 24.13. Gentleman and lady gardeners, with bocage. H: 7". Like the preceding example but with broad bocage fronds. Walton and other potters used this bocage form, so this example cannot be attributed. Price B. *Andrew Dando Antiques.*

Figure 24.14. Gentleman and lady gardeners, reverse of previous example. *Andrew Dando Antiques.*

Figure 24.15. Gentleman and lady gardeners, with bocage. H: ~7.5". Like the preceding example but with different bocage flowers. Walton used this bocage with these flowers, but the bocage alone is not sufficient to support attribution. Price B. *Brighton and Hove Museums.*

Figure 24.16. Gentleman and lady gardeners, with bocage. H: ~7.8". These anthemion-like bocage fronds occur on Walton groups, but are not specific to any pot bank. Price B. *Saffron Walden Museum.*

Figure 24.17. Gentleman and lady gardeners, with bocage. Attributed to Tunstall Group. H: 6.8". The bocage fronds and flowers are typical of the Group. Price B.

Figure 24.18. Gentleman and lady gardeners, with bocage. Attributed to Box Title Group. H: 6.3". Note the typical bocage structure and the green and turquoise colors on the base. A companion group depicts two farm workers. Price B.

Figure 24.19. Gentleman and lady gardeners, with bocage. Attributed to Blue Group. H: 7.2". This group is found in the green palette also used by Blue Group. The lady gardener occurs as a single figure made from the same molds (fig. 24.93). Price A.

Figure 24.20. Gentleman and lady gardener, with vase. Attributed to "Sherratt." H: 7.4". Price B. *Andrew Dando Antiques.*

Figure 24.21. Gentleman gardener with vase. H: 8.3". Pairs with the following vase and is decorated in both enamels and colored glazes. Price C, pair. *The William Herbert and Nancy Hunt Collection.*

Figure 24.22. Gentleman gardener, with vase. H: 7.2". Retains original gilding. Price B. *Peter J. Flemans.*

Figure 24.23. Lady gardener with vase. H: 8.5". Pairs with the previous vase and is decorated in both enamels and colored glazes. Price C, pair. *The William Herbert and Nancy Hunt Collection.*

Figure 24.24. Lady gardener with vase, gentleman gardener with vase, reverse of the previous pair. Similar unpainted creamware vases (not atop plinth bases) at Temple Newsam House (16.79/47) have been attributed to the Leeds Pottery. *The William Herbert and Nancy Hunt Collection.*

Figure 24.25. *GARDENER, & MATE.* Gentleman and lady gardeners, a pair, with bocages. Attributed to "Sherratt." H: 6.3" (L), 6.1" (R). An uncommon pair. Price B.

Figure 24.26. *GARDENER.* Gentleman gardener, with bocage. Attributed to "Sherratt." H: 8.2". His mate on this base is as yet unrecorded. The bocage is restored. Price A.

Figure 24.27. Gentleman and lady gardeners, a pair, with bocages. Attributed to "Sherratt." H: 7.2" (L), 6.7" (R). His bocage is restored. Price A.

Figure 24.28. Gentleman and lady gardeners, a pair, with bocages. Attributed to "Sherratt." H: 6". Price A.

Figure 24.29. *GARDNERS.* Lady gardener, with bocage. Attributed to "Sherratt." H: 5.7". Unlike other "Sherratt" lady gardeners, she is titled *GARDNERS* rather than *MATE.* Price A.

Figure 24.30. Gentleman gardener, with bocage. Attributed to "Sherratt." H: 6". A companion to the preceding figure. Price A.

Figure 24.31. *GARDNERS, GARDNERS*. Lady and gentleman gardeners, a pair, with bocages. Attributed to "Sherratt." H: 5.4". Tiny four-petalled flowers specific to "Sherratt" are on his flower pot and her clothing. The bocage flowers are consistent with the attribution. Price B.

Figure 24.32. *GARDNERS, GARDNERS*, reverse of previous pair. Many potters routinely used bocage fronds of this form, but "Sherratt" used them infrequently.

Figure 24.33. Gentleman and lady gardeners, a pair, with bocages. Attributed to "Sherratt." H: 5.2". The smallest gardener pair from this pot bank. Some bocage restoration. Price A.

Figure 24.34. Gentleman and lady gardeners, a pair, with bocages. H: 4.5" (L), 4.4" (R). These bocages have not been otherwise recorded. The figures' bodies appear to be from the same molds as the bodies of the smallest "Sherratt" gardeners (fig 24.33) and the flowers are like "Sherratt" mayflowers. Price B.

Figure 24.35. Gentleman gardener, with bocage. Impressed "WALTON". H: 5.5". He and his mate are the most common of the three types of gardeners made by Walton. Price A.

Figure 24.36. Lady gardener, with bocage. Impressed "WALTON". H: 5.4". Companion to the preceding figure. Price A.

Figure 24.37. Lady gardener, with bocage. Impressed "WALTON". H: 5.6". From the same molds as the previous figure but differing slightly in the assembly. Price A.

Figure 24.38. Gentleman gardener, with bocage. Impressed "WALTON". H: ~5.7". He and his mate are the next most common of the three types of gardeners made by Walton. Price A.

Figure 24.39. Lady gardener, with bocage. Impressed "WALTON". H: ~5.5". Pairs with preceding figure. Price A.

Figure 24.40. Gentleman gardener, with bocage. Impressed "WALTON". H: ~5.5". He and his mate are the rarest of the three types of gardeners made by Walton. Price A.

Figure 24.41. Lady gardener, with bocage. Impressed "WALTON". H: ~5.5". Pairs with preceding figure. Price A.

Figure 24.42. Lady gardener, with bocage. H: 6.7". Like the lady gardener in the next example, but without a posy in her arm. The color palette is unusual. The bocage has lost one frond. Price A. *William Brook.*

Figure 24.43. Lady gardener, with bocage. H: 6.6". This model is taller than most similarly styled gardeners. The bocage is original and complete. Price A.

Figure 24.44. Gentleman gardener, with bocage. H: 6.6". Companion to the preceding figure. The bocage is restored and probably originally had only one frond to each side. The melon at his feet is more commonly found on figures emblematic of earth. Price A.

Figure 24.45. Gentleman and lady gardeners, a pair, with restored bocages. H: 6.6". Like the preceding larger scale figures, but a pair. Price A.

Figure 24.46. Lady and gentleman gardeners, a pair, with bocages. H: ~5.5". An unusual pair. Price B.

Figure 24.47. Gentleman gardener, with bocage. H: 4.8". These three-leaflet bocage fronds occur on an unclassified Group of figures. Price A.

Figure 24.48. Gentleman gardener, with bocage. H: 4.8". Similar to the previous figure but with the base painted differently. Price A.

Figure 24.49. Gentleman gardener, with bocage. H: 5.1". Similar to the preceding two figures but with a different base. All three figures were presumably made to pair with lady gardeners, but these are unrecorded. Price A.

Figure 24.50. *GARDNERS, GARDNERS.* Lady and gentleman gardeners, a pair, with bocages. Impressed "SALT". H: 5.7" (L), 6" (R). Relatively common gardeners, but marked examples in good condition are difficult to find. Price B.

Figure 24.51. *GARDNERS* (indistinctly titled). Lady gardener, with bocage. Impressed "SALT". H: ~5.7". This example has a very thick bocage, as sometimes occurs on Salt figures. Price A.

Figure 24.52. Gentleman gardener, *GARDNERS*, a pair, with bocages. He attributed to Salt; she impressed "SALT". H: 6" (L), 5.7" (R). The male figure, although unmarked, was almost certainly made by Salt. Price B.

Figure 24.53. Gentleman and lady gardeners, a pair, with bocages. H: ~6". Although unmarked, these closely resemble Salt figures, but resemblance alone cannot support an attribution. Also, blue carnations never appear on marked Salt figures. Price B.

Figure 24.54. Gentleman and lady gardeners, a pair, with bocages. H: 5.7" (L), 5.8" (R). Cannot be attributed to Salt. The heads differ from those on marked Salt figures. Flowers are on the reverse of both bocages, a feature not recorded on marked Salt figures. Price B.

Figure 24.55. Detail of the reverse of the bocage on the previous gentleman gardener, showing flowers on the back of the bocage.

Figure 24.56. *GARDNERS, GARDNERS* (indistinctly titled). Gentleman and lady gardeners, a pair with bocages. Attributed to Daisy Group. H: ~5.5". Price B.

Figure 24.57. *GARDNERS.* Lady gardener, with bocage. H: 5.5". Distinguished from Salt figures of the same form by superior quality, the yellow title area, and different bocage flowers. Price A.

Figure 24.58. Gentleman gardener, with bocage. Attributed to Dudson. H: 4.7". The characteristic bocage supports attribution. Price A.

Figure 24.59. Lady gardener, with bocage. Attributed to Dudson. H: 4.8". A companion to the preceding figure but with a typical brown Dudson base. Price A.

Figure 24.60. *GARDNERS, GARDNERS.* Gentleman and lady gardeners, a pair, with bocages. Attributed to Box Title Group. H: ~6". The carnations are painted in a manner that is typical of this Group. Price B.

Figure 24.61. *GARDNERS, GARDNERS.* Lady and gentleman gardeners, a pair, with bocages. Attributed to Box Title Group. H: ~5.5". Like the previous pair but with the titles painted over. Price B. *Andrew Dando Antiques.*

Figure 24.62. Gentleman and lady gardeners, a pair, with bocages. Attributed to Grape Group. H: 6.5". Price B.

Figure 24.63. Gentleman gardener, with bocage. Attributed to Grape Group. H: 5.5". Price A. *www.madelena.com.*

Figure 24.64. Lady gardener, with bocage. Attributed to Grape Group. H: 6.7". Price A.

Figure 24.65. *GARDNERS*. Gentleman gardener, with bocage. Impressed "HALL". H: 6". The large yellow center of each bocage flower is a Hall feature. Pairs with following figure. Price A.

Figure 24.66. *GARDNERS*. Lady gardener, with bocage. Impressed "HALL". H: ~6". Pairs with the previous figure. The red and blue flowers with large yellow centers occur frequently on Hall figures. Price A.

Figure 24.67. Lady gardener, with bocage. Impressed "HALL". H: 6.1". A blue base is very uncommon on Hall figures. An unusual model in that she holds a flower rather than a watering can. The bocage is restored. Price A.

Figure 24.68. Lady gardener, with bocage. Impressed "HALL". H: 5.5". Bocage restored. The same model as the previous figure but in a more typical palette. Price A. *Michael Goodacre.*

Figure 24.69. Lady gardener, with bocage. Probably made by Hall. H: 5.8". From the same molds as the previous Hall lady gardeners, all having a flower pot rather than a watering can alongside. Her raised hand is restored and should hold a flower. Price A. *Robert Hawker.*

Figure 24.70. Gentleman and lady gardeners, a pair, with bocages. Probably made by Hall. H: 6.3". His oak-leaf bocage with acorns is typical of Hall; hers is restored. She uses the same figure and base molds as figures 24.67–69. Price A.

Figure 24.71. Gentleman gardener, with bocage. Possibly made by Hall. H: 6.2". From the same figure and base molds used for the previous gentleman gardener. Price A.

Figure 24.72. Gentleman and lady gardeners, an assembled pair, with bocages. Probably made by Hall. H: 6" (L), 6.3" (R). The typical Hall bocages are as on the pair in figure 24.70, but the bases and heads differ from those of other Hall figures. See figure 24.54 for another example of this pair of heads. Price A.

Figure 24.73. *GARDNERS.* Gentleman gardener with bocage. Probably made by Hall. H: 6.4". A titled example using Hall's typical oak leaf bocage with acorns. Price A.

Figure 24.74. Lady gardener, with bocage. Attributed to Hall. H: 5.4". The characteristic star bocage flowers are painted in a typical Hall style. The top two bocage fronds are restored. Price A.

Figure 24.75. Lady gardener, with bocage. Attributed to Hall. H: 5.8". Different molds from the previous figure and the watering can tucks beneath her arm. The star bocage flowers support the attribution. The crudeness of the five-leaflet bocage fronds is typical of Hall. Price A. *Robert Hawker.*

Figure 24.76. *GARDNERS.* Gentleman gardener, with bocage. Attributed to Hall. H: ~6". The distinctive six-petalled flowers are specific to Hall. Price A.

Figure 24.77. Gentleman gardener, with bocage. Attributed to Gray Base Group. H: 6.2". Price A.

Figure 24.78. Gentleman gardener, with bocage. Attributed to Straw Flower Group. H: 5.9". The straw flower design is impressed in the base, but much of it is painted green. Price A.

Figure 24.79. Gentleman gardener, with bocage. Attributed to Straw Flower Group. H: 5.9". Pairs with the following figure. Price A.

Figure 24.80. Lady gardener, with bocage. Attributed to Straw Flower Group. H: 5.6". Pairs with the previous figure. Price A.

Figure 24.81. *GARDNERS*. Lady gardener, with bocage. Attributed to Patriotic Group. H: ~ 5.5". Flowers are specific to this Group. Pairs with the following figure. Price A.

Figure 24.82. *GARDINERS*. Gentleman gardener, with bocage. Attributed to Patriotic Group. H: ~ 5.7". Pairs with the previous figure. Price A.

Figure 24.83. Gentleman gardener, with bocage. Attributed to Patriotic Group. H: 5.7". Unlike the previous gentleman gardener from this pot bank, but the bocage flowers support the attribution. Price A.

Figure 24.84. Gentleman gardener, with bocage. Attributed to Tunstall Group. H: 5.9". The bocage has characteristic Tunstall flowers. Pairs with the following figure. Price A. *www.madelena.com.*

Figure 24.85. Lady gardener, with bocage. Attributed to Tunstall Group. H: 5.8". Pairs with the previous figure, but here the bocage flowers are carnations. Price A.

Figure 24.86. Lady gardener, with bocage. Attributed to Tunstall Group. H: 5.8". The bocage flowers are typical of Tunstall. Price A.

Figure 24.87. *GARDNERS* (her title faintly impressed) and gentleman gardener, a pair, with bocages. Attributed to Tunstall Group. H: ~6". Price B. *Nick Burton.*

Figure 24.88. Excavated shard from the High Street, Tunstall, site. The fronds and their arrangement match the bocage on the previous figure. *Image courtesy of The Potteries Museum & Art Gallery, Stoke-on-Trent, UK.*

Figure 24.89. Lady gardener, with bocage. Attributed to Tunstall Group. H: 5.9". Typical Tunstall flowers and blue edging to the bocage fronds. Price A.

Figure 24.90. Lady gardener, with bocage. H: 4.6". Excavated from the Burslem Old Town Hall site associated with Enoch Wood. Of the same form as the lady gardener in the next two pairs. Price A.

Figure 24.91. Lady and gentleman gardeners, a pair, with bocages. Probably made by Enoch Wood. H: ~5.2". Figures using these fragile fern bocage fronds are rarely in good condition. The bocages (with some restoration) match Enoch Wood shards. Price A.

Figure 24.92. Gentleman and lady gardeners, a pair, with bocages. Probably made by Enoch Wood. H: 5.1" (L), 5.4" (R). The bocages (his is restored) comprise hawthorn fronds. Price A.

Figure 24.93. Lady gardener, with bocage. Attributed to Blue Group. H: 5.6". The base and bocage are typical of Blue Group. Price A. *William Brook.*

Figure 24.94. Lady gardener, with bocage. H: 5.2". Each bocage frond comprises three large hawthorn leaves. Price A.

Figure 24.95. Lady gardener, with bocage. H: 5". Similar to the previous figure but with a different base and bocage (with restoration to leaf tips). Price A.

Figure 24.96. Gentleman and lady gardeners, a pair, with bocages. H: 5.1". Unusual examples with particularly attractive bases. Price B.

Figure 24.97. Gentleman gardener, with bocage. H: 5.6". Price A.

Figure 24.98. Lady gardener, with bocage. Attributed to Leather Leaf Group. H: ~6.5". The base and the flowers (only the three fronds to the extreme right are original) support attribution. Price A.

Figure 24.99. Lady gardener, with bocage. Attributed to Leather Leaf Group. H: 6". Similar to the preceding figure but the base was formed without the lower section. The bocage (right side restored) confirms attribution. Price A.

Figure 24.100. Gentleman gardener, with bocage. H: 5.2". A rather crudely made figure. Price A.

Figure 24.101. Lady and gentleman gardeners, a pair, with bocages. H: 5.5" (L), 6.1" (R). A rare pair. A lady archer has the same base and the same bocage fronds, not otherwise recorded (Vol. 2, fig. 84.46). Price B.

Figure 24.102. Gentleman gardener. H: 6". Made without bocage. Price A. *Collection of Arnold and Barbara Berlin.*

Figure 24.103. Gentleman gardener. Impressed "I. DALE BURSLEM". H: 5.1". This figure lost its bocage in the biscuit firing and the stump was glazed and enameled. Price B.

Figure 24.104. *Gardener* and lady holding flowers, a pair. Attributed to Ralph Wood. *Gardener* impressed "1"; lady impressed "2". H: 5.9". Made without bocages. Price B. *Image courtesy of The Potteries Museum & Art Gallery, Stoke-on-Trent, UK.*

Figure 24.105. *Gardener* and lady holding flowers, reverse of previous pair. The back of each base is unpainted and has an impressed number, as occurs on some Ralph Wood figures. *Image courtesy of The Potteries Museum & Art Gallery, Stoke-on-Trent, UK.*

Figure 24.106. *Gardener*. Gentleman gardener. Attributed to Ralph Wood. H: 6". This figure is not numbered, but it is like the previous example impressed "1". Made without bocage. Price A. *Brighton and Hove Museums.*

Figure 24.107. Gardener and lady holding basket of flowers, a pair. H: 4.7". Made without bocages. After the previous Ralph Wood models, but perhaps made around forty years later. Price A. *Michael Grana.*

Figure 24.108. Gentleman gardener. H: 4.5". After the Ralph Wood model. Painted "4" on the rear of the base. Made without bocage. Price A. *www.madelena.com.*

Figure 24.109. Gentleman gardener, with bocage. H: ~4.5". Like the previous example but with a bocage. Price A.

Figure 24.110. *Gardener, & Mate*. Gentleman gardener and lady holding a flower, a pair. Attributed to Ralph Wood. *Gardener* impressed "9"; *& Mate* impressed "8". H: ~8.5". Also occur without numbers or numbered "8" (*Gardener*) and "9" *(& Mate*). Made without bocages. Price B. *John Howard; www.antiquepottery.co.uk.*

Figure 24.111. & *Mate*. Lady holding a flower. Attributed to Ralph Wood; impressed "9". H: ~8.5". Like the previous & *Mate* impressed "8". Made without bocage. Price A. *Image courtesy of The Potteries Museum & Art Gallery, Stoke-on-Trent, UK.*

Figure 24.112. & *Mate.* Lady holding a flower. Attributed to Ralph Wood. H: 8.5". Unnumbered, but like the previous two numbered examples and made without a bocage. Price A.

Figure 24.113. & *Mate, Gardener.* Lady holding flower and gentleman gardener, a pair. Attributed to Ralph Wood. H: 8.5". Like previous Ralph Wood figures but with modified hats. Made without bocages. Price A. *Barbara Gair, www.castle-antiques.com.*

Figure 24.114. & *Mate, Gardener,* reverse of previous pair. As expected of Ralph Wood figures, the bases have rounded internal corners. *Barbara Gair, www.castle-antiques.com.*

Figure 24.115. *Gardener, & Mate.* Gentleman gardener, lady holding flowers. A pair, with bocages. Attributed to Ralph Wood. H: 9". Like the previous pair but with typical Ralph Wood bocages added. Price B. *Wisbech & Fenland Museum.*

Figure 24.116. *Gardener, & Mate,* reverse of previous pair. *Wisbech & Fenland Museum.*

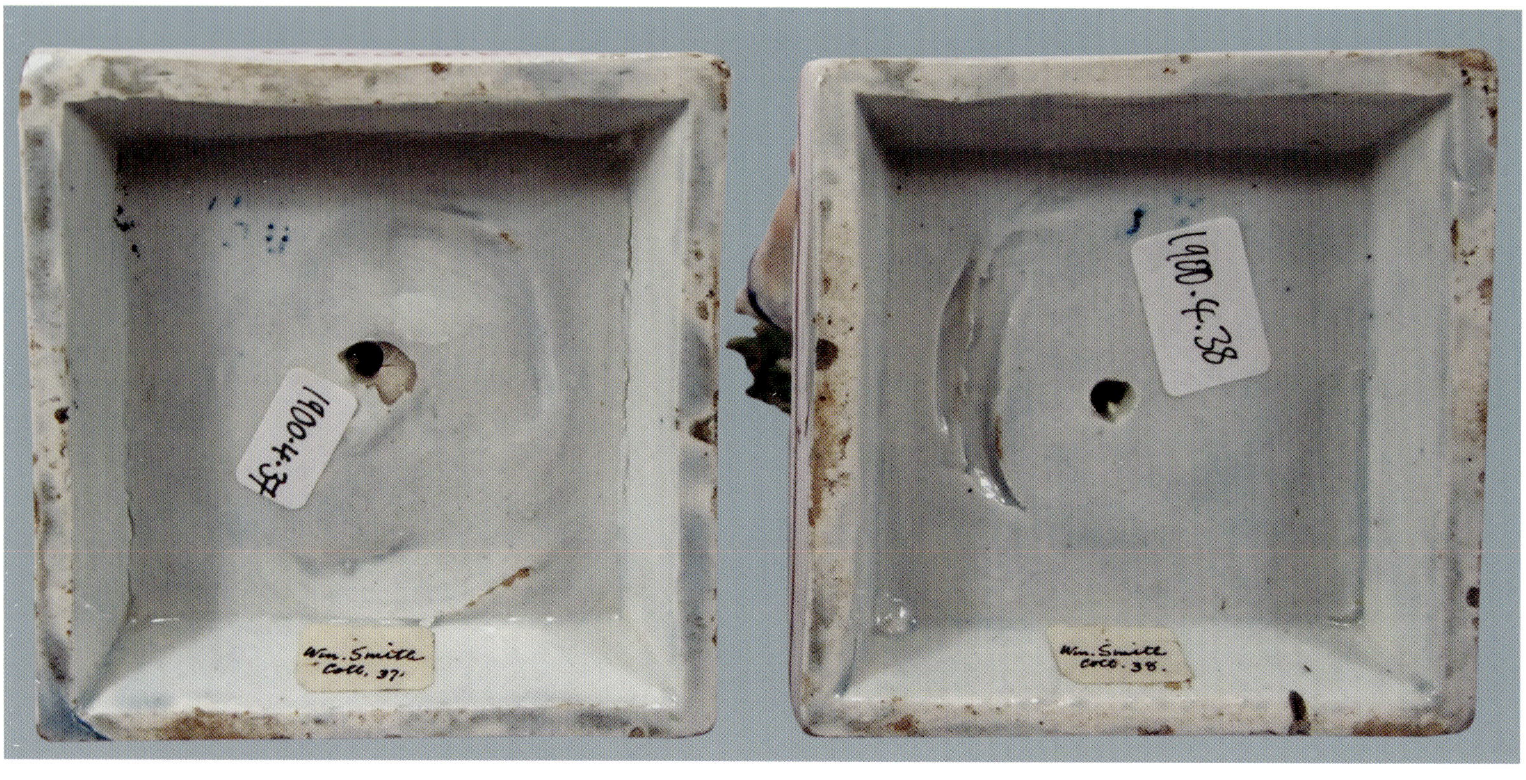

Figure 24.117. Bases of the previous pair of figures of *Gardener* and & *Mate.* Bases with squared internal corners occur on only a handful of Ralph Wood figures. Bases typically have rounded internal corners, and & *Mate* (with bocage) is also recorded formed thus. *Wisbech & Fenland Museum.*

Figure 24.118. Lady holding flowers, with bocage. Attributed to Ralph Wood. H: ~9". From the same molds as previous similar figures but untitled. Price A. *Martyn Edgell Antiques Ltd.*

Figure 24.119. *Gardener*. Gentleman gardener, with bocage. Attributed to Ralph Wood. H: 8.5". The hat differs from that on the Ralph Wood *Gardener* impressed "9". Pairs with the following figure, both having the muddier palette and large titling associated with some Ralph Wood figures. Price A. *Richard Montgomery.*

Figure 24.120. *Mate*. Lady holding flowers, with bocage. Attributed to Ralph Wood. H: 8.9". Pairs with the previous *Gardener*. Like previously shown Ralph Wood & *Mate* figures, but the hat differs from the hat on figures impressed "8" and "9". Price A. *Image courtesy of The Potteries Museum & Art Gallery, Stoke-on-Trent, UK.*

Figure 24.121. Gentleman gardener and lady holding flowers, a pair. Attributed to Dudson. H: 8.3" (L), 9.2" (R). The figures seem to be from the same molds as previous Ralph Wood pairs. The x-sprigs at her feet are specific to Dudson. Made without bocages. Price A. *Sheila Wilson.*

Figure 24.122. Gentleman gardener. H: 8.3". Made without bocage. After the Ralph Wood gentleman gardener, previously shown. Restoration to his right arm, spade, and plume on hat. Price A. *Whitehall Antiques, Chapel Hill, North Carolina.*

Figure 24.123. Girl with flower, with bocage. H: ~6". Companion to the following figure. Price A. *Andrew Dando Antiques.*

Figure 24.124. Boy with flower, with bocage. H: ~6". Companion to the previous figure. Price A. *Andrew Dando Antiques.*

Figure 24.125. Girl with flower, with bocage. Probably made by Dale. H: 6.5". The flowers on the bocage are of a type used only by Dale and Tittensor. Price A.

Figure 24.126. Girl with flower, with bocage. H: 6.2". Price A.

Figure 24.127. Girl with flower, with bocage. Attributed to Dudson. H: 5.8". She holds a typical Dudson x-sprig. The bocage is restored. Price A.

Figure 24:128. Boy with flower, girl, a pair, with bocages. Attributed to Ralph Wood. H: 5.5". Typical Ralph Wood bases, bocages, and decoration. No examples of these figures with impressed numbers are known. Price A. *Michael Goodacre.*

Figure 24.129. Detail of the typical Ralph Wood bocage on the previous figure of a boy. *Michael Goodacre.*

Figure 24.130. Boy with flower, with bocage. Attributed to Ralph Wood. H: ~6.5". The bocage and the line banding three sides of the base are typical of Ralph Wood. The muddier palette and black line on the base are consistent with the attribution. Price A.

Figure 24.131. Boy with flower, with bocage. H: 6.8". The bocage is not original to the figure, but such five-leaflet bocage fronds have been noted on similar examples of the figure. Price A.

Figure 24.132. Gentleman with bird's nest, lady with flower (now lost). Possibly made by Enoch Wood. H: 5.5" (L); 5.8" (R). A rare pair of figures. Made without bocages. The thick-walled bases are suggestive of an Enoch Wood origin. Price B. *Brighton and Hove Museums.*

Figure 24.133. Lady with flower, with bocage. Attributed to Patriotic Group. H: 6.2". The pinecone bocage is specific to Patriotic Group. The girl appears to be from the same molds as the girl in figure 24.132. Note the gilding on her shoes. Price B.

Figure 24.134. Lady with flowers. H: ~5.5". Made without bocage. Price A.

Figure 24.135. Lady with flowers. H: 5.5". Made without bocage. Price A. *Elinor Penna.*

Figure 24.136. Lady with flower. H: 6". Made without bocage. Price A. *Andrew Dando Antiques.*

Figure 24.137. Lady with flower. H: 6.1". Made without bocage. Price A.

Figure 24.138. Lady with flower. Attributed to Gray Base Group. H: 6.2". Made without bocage. The strong glazes and bright enamels are typical of this Group. Price A.

Figure 24.139. Lady with flowers. Attributed to Gray Base Group. H: 6.1". Made without bocage. The figure, including the mound on the base, is from the same molds as that used for the previous example, and Gray Base Group bases are sometimes black. Price A.

Figure 24.140. Lady with flowers. H: 6". Made without bocage. Price A. *Elinor Penna.*

Figure 24.141. Lady with flowers. H: 5.4". Made without bocage. Price A. *Jack Hardin.*

Figure 24.142. Lady with flowers. H: ~6". Made without bocage. Price A. *Elinor Penna.*

Figure 24.143. Lady with flowers. H: 4.8". Made without bocage. Price A. *Kevin Stafford.*

Figure 24.144. Gardener with spade, lady with flower, each standing alongside a plinth with a potted plant atop, a pair. H: 4.5". Rare figures. Made without bocages. Price C. *Photograph Courtesy of Sotheby's, Inc. © 2013.*

25. Reading

In the early 1800s, feeble improvements in England's ramshackle educational system coupled with an ever-growing supply of affordable reading matter resulted in the explosive growth of the reading public. Children were not the only new readers. Many uneducated adults strove to acquire reading skills. Homes proudly displaying earthenware figures of people absorbed in books proclaimed the family's status as educated members of society.

Figure 25.1. Reading maid, with bocage. Attributed to "Sherratt." H: 10.6". This figure occurs only rarely on this particularly pretty rainbow base. The base, the bocage, and the floral sprigs at the maid's feet are typical of "Sherratt." Price B.

Figure 25.2. *VILAGE MAID*, with bocage. Attributed to "Sherratt." H: ~11.5". Like the previous figure but on a typical "Sherratt" table base. Charming misspelling is common on figures because many in the Potteries were semi-literate. Price B. *Collection of Michael J. Smith.*

Figure 25.3. *THE READING MAID,* with bocage. Attributed to "Sherratt." H: ~11.5". Like the previous figures but on a different typical "Sherratt" base. "Sherratt" used the titles *THE READING MAID* and *VILLAGE MAID* interchangeably for this figure. Price B.

Figure 25.4. *THE READING MAID,* with bocage. Attributed to "Sherratt." H: ~11.5". Like the previous figure, but the bocage (largely restored) is arranged in an arc, as sometimes occurs on "Sherratt" figures. The dress color and pattern are atypical of "Sherratt." Price B.

Figure 25.5. Reading maid, with bocage. Attributed to "Sherratt." H: 11.6". Like the previous examples but untitled. Price B.

Figure 25.6. Reading maid, seated between two columns. Attributed to "Sherratt." H: 9.6". An arch topped by a cherub once spanned this figure. The feathered base and the floral sprigs applied to the mound near her feet are characteristic of "Sherratt." Price A. *Elinor Penna.*

Figure 25.7. Reading maid. Attributed to "Sherratt." H: 9.3". Made without bocage. The floral sprigs applied to the mound are specific to "Sherratt". Price B. *Andrew Dando Antiques.*

Figure 25.8. Reading maid, with bocage. Attributed to "Sherratt." H: 11". Like the previous figure but with some bocage. Price A. *Barbara Gair; www.castle-antiques.com.*

Figure 25.9. Reading maid, with umbrella, with bocage. H: 10". This large lass, known from only this figure, is the only large reading maid not attributable to "Sherratt." Price B. *Élinor Penna.*

Figure 25.10. Lady reading, with cat and lamb, with bocage. Attributed to Patriotic Group. H: 8.5". The bocage and sprigs on the base are typical of the Group. The small cat (rather than a dog) is unusual and occurs in other examples from this pot bank. Price B. *Richard Montgomery.*

Figure 25.11. Lady reading, with cat, with bocage. Attributed to Patriotic Group. H: ~8.5". Like the previous example in that there are characteristic sprigs on the base, but the bocage differs. This lady occurs within other groups attributable to Patriotic Group. Price B.

Figure 25.12. Gentleman with a book, dog, and lamb, lady reading with a cat and lamb. A pair, with bocages. H: ~9". Attributed to Patriotic Group. Like other examples from this Group, these display characteristic bocages and floral sprigs. Price B.

Figure 25.13. Gentleman with book, with dog and lamb, with bocage. Attributed to Patriotic Group. H: ~8.5". Companion subject to the previous two figures of ladies. Like the previous gentleman, but the book and hat have switched places. Price B.

Figure 25.14. Lady reading, with cat, with bocage. Marked "WALTON" in raised letters. H: 5.8". The only marked Walton subject that includes a small cat. Also made in porcelain, similarly marked and without a bocage (The Potteries Museum). Price B.

Figure 25.15. Lady reading, with cat, with spill vase. Marked "WALTON". H: ~5.8". Like the previous figure but with a spill vase. Price B.

Figure 25.16. Lady reading, with cat, with bocage. Made by Walton and marked with the ribbon associated with the Walton mark with raised letters, but the lettering is illegible. H: ~6". Pairs with a sportsman with dog, also with an arc bocage (Vol. 2, fig. 84.61). Price B. *Collection of Susan and Richard Cann.*

Figure 25.17. Boy reading, with bocage. Impressed "TITTENSOR". H: 7". Restoration to left of bocage. These twelve-petalled bocage flowers occur only on two other marked Tittensor bocage figures and on Dale figures. Price B.

Figure 25.18. Boy reading, reverse of previous figure. The impressed "TITTENSOR" mark is about two-thirds up the green stump, and the rectangular area around it is unpainted.

Figure 25.19. Lady reading, with bocage. H: 6". Note the very large book. Price B.

Figure 25.20. Lady reading, with bocage. H: ~6". Like the previous figure but with oak-leaf bocage fronds. Price A.

Figure 25.21. *READING BOY,* with bocage. Attributed to Box Title Group. H: 6". A pair titled in the same style is recorded, with both figures having bocage flowers painted in a manner typical of the Group. Price A.

Figure 25.22. Boy and girl reading, an assembled pair, with bocages. Probably made by Dale. H: ~6" (L), ~6.2" (R). The twelve-petalled flowers on her bocage only appear on Dale and Tittensor figures, and his bocage is consistent with a Dale attribution. Price B.

Figure 25.23. Boy and girl reading, an assembled pair, with bocages. Attributed to Leather Leaf Group. H: ~6.5". Heads are molded differently to those of the previous pair. The flowers on the bases and bocages are characteristic of this Group. Price B.

Figure 25.24. Boy reading, with bocage. Attributed to Leather Leaf Group. H: 7.5". The bocage leaves, the acorns on the bocage, and the base are typical of this Group. The boy's head is from the same molds used for the boy's head in the previous pair. Price B. *Peter Flemans.*

Figure 25.25. Boy reading, with bocage. Attributed to Leather Leaf Group. H: 7.5". Like the previous boy but painted differently. Price A.

Figure 25.26. Boy and girl reading, a pair. Attributed to Leather Leaf Group. H: 6" (L), 6.2" (R). The flowers on the bases support the attribution. Made without bocages. Price B. *Elinor Penna.*

Figure 25.27. Lady reading, with bocage. H: ~7.5". This figure's gray hair and the painting of her clothing to her neckline have transformed what would otherwise be a reading maid into a mature lady. Price A. *Barbara Gair; www.castle-antiques.com.*

Figure 25.28. Boy and girl reading, a pair, with bocages. H: ~6.2". Price B. *John Howard; www.antiquepottery.co.uk.*

Figure 25.29. Girl reading. H: 6". Made without bocage. Price A.

Figure 25.30. Girl reading. H: 6.6". Made without bocage. Price A. *Barbara Gair; www.castle-antiques.com.*

Figure 25.31. Boy reading. H: ~6.1". Made without bocage. Price A.

Figure 25.32. *COTTAGE BOY, COTTAGE GIRL.* Girl and boy reading, a pair. H: ~6.5" (L), ~6.7" (R). Made without bocages. Like previous examples but titled. A female figure mistitled *COTTAGE BOY* has been recorded. Price B. *John Howard; www.antiquepottery.co.uk.*

Figure 25.33. Boy reading. H: 6.7". Like previous examples but painted in a different manner. Seemingly identical figures can differ by up to 10% in size because shrinkage rates during firing vary. Price A. *Elinor Penna.*

Figure 25.34. Girl and boy reading, a pair. H: 5.6" (L), 5.8" (R). Made without bocages and without the rectangular bases on previous similar examples. Price B. *John Howard; www.antiquepottery.co.uk.*

Figure 25.35. Boy and girl reading, a pair. H: 6.5" (L), 6" (R). Made without bocages and without rectangular bases. Price A. *Peter Flemans.*

Figure 25.36. *VILLAGE GIRL, VILLAGE BOY.* Girl and boy reading, a pair. H: ~6.4". Made without bocages. From different molds than those used for previous examples. Price B.

Figure 25.37. *VILLAGE GIRL.* Girl reading. H: 6.4". Made without bocage. Not from the same molds as the previous *VILLAGE GIRL.* Price A. *Barbara Gair; www.castle-antiques.com.*

Figure 25.38. Girl reading. H: 5.5". This figure probably had a lid atop the urn and functioned as an inkstand. A rare figure. Price B.

Figure 25.39. Girl reading. H: 6". Like the previous example but with a different base. The base occurs on a small boy pushing a barrel (fig. 29.32). Price B. *Collection of Arnold and Barbara Berlin.*

Figure 25.40. Dame school. H: 6". A dame school, run in the home of an elderly dame or gentleman, taught basic reading and domestic skills to the young children of the working poor. The dame holds a broom on her lap. Price C.

Figure 25.41. Dame school. H: 6". Dame schools are uncommon. Placement of the benches varies from example to example. Price C. *Philip Carrol.*

Figure 25.42. Girl reading, with spill vase. H: 7.3". Price A.

Figure 25.43. Girl reading. L: 6.5". Price B. *Woolley and Wallis Salisbury Salerooms Ltd.*

Figure 25.44. Girl reading. L: ~6.5". Price A.

Figure 25.45. Girl reading, with boy, with spill vase. H: ~5". Price A.

Figure 25.46. Boy reading. Possibly made by Dale. H: 3.2". Made without bocage. The flower on the base and the facial features are typical of Dale. Price A.

Figure 25.47. Boy reading. Possibly made by Dale. H: 3.2". Made without bocage. Has the same flower as the previous figure. In both, the book and hands, although placed differently, are unrestored. Price A. *John Howard; www.antiquepottery.co.uk.*

Figure 25.48. Boy reading. H: 3.2". Made without bocage. Pairs with the following girl. Price A.

Figure 25.49. Girl reading. H: 3.2". Made without bocage. Pairs with the previous boy. Price A. *Michael Goodacre.*

Figure 25.50. Girl reading. H: 3.2". Made without bocage. Like the previous girl but with a three-leaflet frond of the type normally found on bocages of finer figures, here applied to the base. Price A. *Peter Flemans.*

Figure 25.51. Boy holding book, with bocage. Attributed to "Sherratt." H: 4.9". This figure is from the same molds as one of the figures flanking large *PREPARE TO MEET THY GOD* groups. The companion figure, a boy holding a sword, also occurs on this base (Volume 2, fig. 79.35). Price A.

Figure 25.52. Boy holding book, boy holding sword. An assembled pair, with bocages. Attributed to "Sherratt." H: 5". The boy with the book is like the previous figure but on a different base. Price A. *Eileen and Robert Carde.*

Figure 25.53. Girl reading, with bocage. Attributed to "Sherratt." H: 4.8". The floral sprigs applied to the base are characteristic of "Sherratt," and the bocage and base are consistent with the attribution. Price B.

Figure 25.54. Girl reading, reverse of previous figure showing five-leaflet fern fronds. Price B.

Figure 25.55. Boy and girl reading, with bocage. Attributed to "Sherratt." H: ~5". The same girl and five-leaflet fern fronds as in the previous example. Price B.

Figure 25.56. Boy and girl reading, with bocage. Attributed to "Sherratt." H: ~5". Like the previous example but with a different bocage (double anthemion fronds) that is consistent with the attribution. Price B.

Figure 25.57. Boy and girl reading, with bocage. Attributed to "Sherratt." H: 5.3". Like the previous examples and on a typical "Sherratt" base. The bocage is largely restored, as are the outstretched arms and the books. Price A.

Figure 25.58. Girl holding a flower with boy reading, with bocage. Attributed to "Sherratt." H: ~5". The same figures as in previous examples but with the figures switched. Here the five-leaflet fern fronds are arranged in an arc. Price B.

Figure 25.59. Girl holding a flower with boy reading, with bocage. Attributed to "Sherratt." H: ~5". Like previous examples. The floral sprigs applied to the base are specific to "Sherratt." Price B.

Figure 25.60. Boy and girl reading, a pair, with bocages. Attributed to "Sherratt." H: ~5". The bases and bocages support the attribution. Price A.

Figure 25.61. *GOOD BOY, GOOD GIRL* (titles impressed on fronts of bases). Boy and girl reading, a pair. Impressed "SALT". H: 3". Price B. *Andrew Dando Antiques.*

Figure 25.62. *GOOD BOY, GOOD GIRL*, reverse of previous pair showing the impressed "SALT" marks. *Andrew Dando Antiques.*

Figure 25.63. *GOOD GIRL*. Girl reading. Impressed "SALT". H: 3". Like the girl in the previous pair but more simply painted. Price A.

Figure 25.64. Boy reading. H: 3.2". Price A.

Figure 25.65. Girl reading. H: 3". Price A. *Collection of Michael J. Smith.*

Figure 25.66. Girl and boy reading, a pair. H: 2.9". Price A. *Aurea Carter Antiques.*

Figure 25.67. Girl reading. H: 2.2". Such tiny figures ooze disproportionate charm. Price A.

26. Music

Music has been integral to the fabric of English life throughout modern history, and tambourines, triangles, pipes, fiddles, tabors, guitars, horns, and a host of simple musical instruments were an established source of pleasure in the pre-Victorian decades. In particular, the genre of dance music transcended all class boundaries because country dancing was equally popular at aristocratic balls and rural celebrations. Some Staffordshire figure groups give glimpses of the polished musicians who entertained devotees of sophisticated music, but most groups portray traditional entertainers who delighted people of all classes.

Figure 26.1. Gentleman piper, lady lute player, a pair, both with dogs. H: ~4.9" (L), 5.2" (R). Made without bocages. These figures also occur with yellow rather than green bases. Price B.

Figure 26.2. Lady lute player, gentleman piper, a pair, both with dogs. H: 5.2" (L), 4.9" (R). Like the previous pair and made without bocages. Resemble "Sherratt" figures, but an attribution cannot be supported. Price B.

Figure 26.3. Lady lute player, with sheep, with bocage. Possibly made by Dale. H: ~4.5". The bocage and its flowers are in the style of Dale. A companion to the following figure. Price B.

Figure 26.4. Gentleman piper with dog, with bocage. Possibly made by Dale. H: 4.5". A companion to the previous figure. Price B.

Figure 26.5. Gentleman piper with dog and sheep, with bocage. Attributed to Leaf Mat Group. H: 4.9". Unusual in that the bocage frond is not paired back-to-back with another. Price B.

Figure 26.6. Lady lute player with sheep, gentleman piper with sheep and dog, a pair, with bocages. Attributed to "Sherratt." H: 4.9" (L), 5.1" (R). Typical "Sherratt" bocages and flowers. Price B.

Figure 26.7. Lady lute player, gentleman piper, reverse of previous pair.

Figure 26.8. Lady lute player with sheep, with bocage. Attributed to "Sherratt." H: 4.9". Like the previous lute player but with different bocage flowers. Price A.

Figure 26.9. Gentleman piper with dog and sheep, with bocage. Attributed to "Sherratt." H: 4.9". Similar to the piper in the preceding pair, but the sheep are not modeled separately and are instead integral to the base. Price A.

Figure 26.10. Lady lute player with sheep, with bocage. Attributed to "Sherratt." H: 4.3". A companion to the preceding piper and similarly has two sheep integral to the base. Price A.

Figure 26.11. Lady lute player with sheep, with bocage. Attributed to "Sherratt." H: 4.8". A similar lady to those in previous examples but seated on a waisted base. Restored bocage. Price A.

Figure 26.12. Gentleman holding horn, with dog, with bocage. Attributed to "Sherratt." H: 4.8". The same gentleman as in previous "Sherratt" examples but now seated within an arc bocage. Price A.

Figure 26.13. Lady lute player and gentleman piper, with sheep and dog, with bocage. Attributed to "Sherratt." H: 4.7". The same lady and gentleman as in the preceding "Sherratt" examples. Price B.

Figure 26.14. Gentleman piper with dog and sheep, lady lute player with sheep, a pair, with bocages. Attributed to "Sherratt." H: 6.2" (L), 5.8" (R). Price B.

Figure 26.15. Gentleman piper, lady lute player with sheep, a pair, with bocages. Attributed to "Sherratt." H: 4.8" (L), 5.5" (R). These figures are from the same molds as the standing couple in the preceding example. The only known pair. With losses. Price B. *Brighton and Hove Museums.*

Figure 26.16. Gentleman piper and lady lute player, with dog and sheep, with bocage. Attributed to "Sherratt." H: 6.1". Pink luster decoration is typical of "Sherratt." Bocage restored. Price A.

Figure 26.17. Gentleman piper with sheep, with bocage. Attributed to "Sherratt." H: 4.6". "Sherratt" often used this bocage with a turquoise palette. The companion figure is a lady holding a sheep (fig. 27.106). Price B.

Figure 26.18. Lady holding a sheep and gentleman playing a horn, with sheep, with bocage. Attributed to "Sherratt." H: ~4.5". The gentleman is the same figure as in the preceding example. Price B.

Figure 26.19. Lady holding a lamb and gentleman piper, with sheep and a dog, with bocage. Attributed to "Sherratt." H: ~4.8". Similar to the previous example. Unlike all preceding "Sherratt" lady musicians, she does not have a floral dress. Price B. *Elinor Penna.*

Figure 26.20. Lady holding a sheep and gentleman piper, with bocage. Attributed to "Sherratt." H: 4.9". The same figures as in preceding examples with a typical "Sherratt" base and bocage. Price B.

Figure 26.21. Exotically attired piper. Attributed to "Sherratt." H: 3.7". Made without bocage. This figure occurs on "Sherratt" menageries and trumpet spill vases. The double-lined base is typical of "Sherratt." Like figures 26.22–25, it is rare. Price A.

Figure 26.22. Lady with tambourine. Attributed to "Sherratt." H: 4.3". Made without bocage. This figure occurs on "Sherratt" menageries and, in one recorded instance, on a trumpet spill vase. Also found on the double-lined square base seen on the following figure. Price A.

Figure 26.23. Gentleman with barrel organ. Attributed to "Sherratt." H: ~4.4". This figure occurs on "Sherratt" menageries and, in one recorded instance, on a trumpet spill vase. Price A.

Figure 26.24. Gentleman with barrel organ. Attributed to "Sherratt." H: 4.4". Made without bocage. Like the previous figure but on a "Sherratt" red, white, and blue base. Price A.

Figure 26.25. Gentleman with fiddle. Attributed to "Sherratt." H: 4.7". Made without bocage. Unlike figures 26.21–24, this figure does not occur on menageries. Here it is on a typical "Sherratt" red, white, and blue base. Price A.

Figure 26.26. Shepherd piper with sheep, with bocage. Attributed to Big Blossom Group. H: 5". Price B.

Figure 26.27. Shepherd piper with sheep and a goat, with bocage. H: 5.3". The bocage and the animals differ from those on the previous rather similar example. Price B.

Figure 26.28. Shepherd piper with sheep, with bocage. H: ~5". A different bocage and flock of animals to previous similar examples. Price B. *Collection of Michael J. Smith.*

Figure 26.29. Shepherd piper with sheep, with bocage. H: ~5". The same theme as the previous three examples. Such groups are uncommon. Despite their similarities, each has a quite different bocage. Price B. *Andrew Dando Antiques.*

Figure 26.30. Shepherd piper with sheep, reverse of previous example. *Andrew Dando Antiques.*

Figure 26.31. *GUITAR PLAYER.* Lady with guitar, with bocage. Impressed "I. DALE BURSLEM". H: 4.4". Pairs with the following *PIPE PLAYER.* Both are rare. Price B.

Figure 26.32. *PIPE PLAYER.* Gentleman piper, with bocage. Impressed "I. DALE BURSLEM". H: 4.6". Pairs with the previous *GUITAR PLAYER.* Price B.

Figure 26.33. *GUITAR PLAYER, PIPE PLAYER,* reverse of previous pair. The apple green painting and rows of tooth-like indentations on the bases are typical of Dale. Both figures are well marked.

Figure 26.34. Lady lute player, gentleman piper, each among sheep, a pair, with bocages. H: 4.2" (L), 4.4" (R). The figures differ slightly from the previous Dale pair. Dale used bocage flowers of this form on some of his figures, but the Dale flowers are usually larger. Price B.

Figure 26.35. Gentleman piper, lady lute player, each among sheep, a pair, with bocages. Attributed to Blue Group. H: 4.3". From the same figure and base molds as the previous pair. The back of each bocage is unpainted, and the bocages support the attribution. Price B.

Figure 26.36. Lady lute player among sheep, with bocage. H: 4.5". In the style of the Blue Group, but attribution is not possible. Price A. *Andrew Dando Antiques.*

Figure 26.37. Lady lute player among sheep, reverse of previous figure showing the unpainted bocage, in the style of the Blue Group. *Andrew Dando Antiques.*

Figure 26.38. Gentleman piper among sheep, with bocage. Attributed to Box Title Group. H: 4.4". The painting of the bocage flowers, the turquoise and green base, and the quality of the glazes support the attribution. Price A. *Image courtesy of The Potteries Museum & Art Gallery, Stoke-on-Trent, UK.*

Figure 26.39. Gentleman piper among sheep, with bocage. H: ~4.5". Like previous pipers, but the bocage is different. Price A.

Figure 26.40. Gentleman piper, lady lute player, each among sheep, a pair, with bocages. H: ~4.2". These figures are from the same molds as used for the previous pairs of figures on this theme. His bocage is restored. Price A.

Figure 26.41. Lady lute player, with bocage. Impressed "I. DALE BURSLEM". H: 4.8". A rare figure. The following unmarked piper is probably her companion. Price A.

Figure 26.42. Lady lute player, reverse of previous example with "I. DALE BURSLEM" impressed.

Figure 26.43. Gentleman piper, with bocage. Attributed to Dale. H: 5.4". The bocage flowers are typical of Dale, as is the man's fat face. The base and its scrolling are closely similar to that of the preceding guitar player, which presumably was modeled to pair with this figure. Price A.

Figure 26.44. Lady lute player with sheep, with bocage. Attributed to Dale. H: 5.8". The flowers on the base are characteristic of Dale. The lady is from the same molds as figure 26.41. Price A.

Figure 26.45. Gentleman piper and lady lute player, a pair, each with a sheep and spill vase. Attributed to Dale. H: 5.8". These are the same lady and gentleman as in the preceding Dale examples. The floral sprigs on their bases confirm the attribution. Price B.

Figure 26.46. Gentleman piper with dog, sheep, and spill vase. H: 7.6". Price B.

Figure 26.47. Gentleman piper with dog, sheep, and spill vase. H: 7.5". Like the preceding example but with a rare black sheep. Price B.

Figure 26.48. Gentleman bagpiper with sheep and a floral spill vase. H: ~6". A companion to the following example and from the same pot bank. Price A. *Andrew Dando Antiques.*

Figure 26.49. Gentleman piper with sheep, dog, and a floral spill vase. H: 6". The piper's hands and pipe are restored, and he may originally have held a tabor. Price A.

Figure 26.50. Gentleman with tabor, with dog, swan, and vine-covered spill vase. Probably made by Ralph Wood. H: ~6". The man is from the same molds as the tabor player on a *Rurel-Paftime* group attributed to Ralph Wood (fig. 26.92), and the pastel palette is typical of Ralph Wood. Price A. *Collection of Arnold and Barbara Berlin.*

Figure 26.51. Gentleman bagpiper with swan and squirrel, with vine-covered spill vase. Probably made by Ralph Wood. H: 6.5". The bagpiper is from the same molds as the bagpiper on the Ralph Wood *Rural Pastime* group impressed "166" (fig. 26.91). The palette on the base is typical of Ralph Wood. Price A. *Collection of Arnold and Barbara Berlin.*

Figure 26.52. Gentleman bagpiper with dog, swan, and vine-covered spill vase. H: 6". Similar to the previous example but lacking Ralph Wood features. Price A. *Whitehall Antiques, Chapel Hill, North Carolina.*

Figure 26.53. A pair of spill vases, one with a gentleman bagpiper, the other with a gentleman with a tabor, each with a dog and swan. H: 6". The vase with a bagpiper is similar to the previous example, but the bagpiper now sits on the opposite side of the vase. Price A.

Figure 26.54. Gentleman bagpiper with sheep, owl, and spill vase. H: ~6". Price A. *Collection of Arnold and Barbara Berlin.*

Figure 26.55. Gentleman bagpiper with dog and spill vase. H: ~6". An unusual variation on a standard theme. Price A. *Andrew Dando Antiques.*

Figure 26.56. Gentleman bagpiper with spill vase, reverse of previous example. *Andrew Dando Antiques.*

Figure 26.57. Gentleman bagpiper and lady, with squirrel and spill vase. H: 6.2", L: 6.5". Pairs with the following vase. Price C, pair. *The William Herbert and Nancy Hunt Collection.*

Figure 26.58. Lady holding a stick and gentleman horn player, with dog. H: 6.2", L: 6.5". Pairs with the previous vase. Price C, pair. *The William Herbert and Nancy Hunt Collection.*

Figure 26.59. A pair of spill vases, one with a gentleman piper and lady, the other with a gentleman bagpiper and lady, both with sheep. H: 5.7" (L), 5.5" (R). Like the previous two vases but with sheep in place of the other animals. Price B. *Image courtesy of The Potteries Museum & Art Gallery, Stoke-on-Trent, UK.*

Figure 26.60. Gentleman bagpiper and lady lute player, with sheep, goat, and dog, with bocage. Possibly attributable to Box Title Group. H: ~8". The painting of the carnations and the glaze suggest the attribution. Price B.

Figure 26.61. Lady lute player and gentleman flautist, with sheep and swan, with bocage. Probably attributable to Box Title Group. H: ~8". Untitled, but the color palette on the base, the structure of the bocage, and the bocage flowers support attribution. May be a companion to the previous example. Price B.

Figure 26.62. Lady lute player and gentleman flautist, with sheep and swan, with bocage. H: 8.2". Similar in composition to the previous example. Competing pot banks potted look-alikes of each other's work, and this example lacks features to support attribution. Price B.

Figure 26.63. Lady lute player and gentleman flautist, with sheep and swan, with bocage. Attributed to Big Blossom Group. H: ~9". Price B.

Figure 26.64. Lady lute player and gentleman flautist, with sheep and swan, with bocage. H: 8". The swan's head and neck are bent to attach to its breast, and this has protected them from damage. Price B.

Figure 26.65. Gentleman bagpiper and lady lute player, with dog and sheep, with bocage. H: 8.7". Note the strong, bright enamels and glaze. Price B.

Figure 26.66. Gentleman bagpiper and lady lute player, with dog, goat, and sheep, with bocage. H: 10.5". These three-leaflet bocage fronds routinely occur on an array of unclassified figures that are probably from the same pot bank. Price B. *Rago Arts and Auction Center, Lambertville, New Jersey.*

Figure 26.67. Lady lute player with dog and gentleman flautist (flute lost), with swans, with bocage. H: 10". Companion subject to the preceding example. Both have three-leaflet bocage fronds, but the flowers differ. Price B. *Peter Flemans.*

Figure 26.68. Lady lute player and gentleman flautist, with swans, with bocage. H: 9.8". These musicians occur with various bocage forms, and here the bocage has five-leaflet fronds. Price B.

Figure 26.69. Lady lute player with dog, gentleman flautist, with swans, with bocage. H: ~10.5". Similar in composition to previous examples. Companion subject to the following example. Both are in the style of Walton but were probably made by some other potter. Price B. *Elinor Penna.*

Figure 26.70. Gentleman bagpiper and lady lute player, with dog, goat, and sheep, with bocage. H: ~10.5". The plumes atop the figures' heads are formed as bocage leaves. Companion to the previous group. Price B. *Collection of Susan and Richard Cann.*

Figure 26.71. Gentleman bagpiper and lady lute player, reverse of previous example showing the very full bocage. Price B. *Collection of Susan and Richard Cann.*

Figure 26.72. Gentleman bagpiper and lady lute player, with dog, goat, and sheep, with bocage. H: 9.7". Similar to the previous example, but the recumbent sheep and the goat have exchanged places. Again, bocage leaves are painted to simulate the plumes atop the figures' heads. Price B.

Figure 26.73. Gentleman bagpiper and lady lute player, with dog, goat, and sheep, with bocage. H: ~9". Price B.

Figure 26.74. Gentleman bagpiper and lady lute player, with goat and sheep, with bocage. H: 9". Unusually bold flowers are on the bocage. Price B.

Figure 26.75. Gentleman bagpiper, lady lute player, with dog, goat, and sheep, with bocage. H: ~9.5". Walton and other pot banks occasionally used these dramatic bocage leaves. Price B.

Figure 26.76. *VILLAGE GROUP.* Lady tambourine player and gentleman bugler, with bocage. Attributed to Box Title Group. Box Title bocages often have spindly branches. H: 7.8". Price B. *Peter Flemans.*

Figure 26.77. *VILLAGE GROUP.* Gentleman bagpiper and lady with triangle, with bocage. Attributed to Box Title Group. H: 7.3". Companion to the previous example. Price B.

Figure 26.78. Gentleman piper and lady lute player, with bocage. Attributed to Dale. H: 8.6". The bocage, the twelve-petalled flowers, and the figures' plump faces support the attribution. A companion to the following example. Price B.

Figure 26.79. Lady with tambourine and gentleman playing horn, with bocage. Attributed to Dale. H: 9.2". Companion to the preceding group. The striking flowers on the bases are not specific to Dale. Price B.

Figure 26.80. Gentleman playing horn and songstress. H: 8.4". The bocage fronds are not paired back-to-back with others. Price B. *John Howard; www.antiquepottery.co.uk.*

Figure 26.81. *VILLAGE GROUP.* Lady lute player and gentleman piper, with bocage. Attributed to Tunstall Group. H: 7.5". The bocage, the flowers, and the yellow title area are typical of "Tunstall." The pipe is restored and originally may have been a horn. Price B.

Figure 26.82. *VILLAGE GROUP.* Lady with tambourine and gentleman bugler, with bocage. Attributed to Tunstall Group. H: 7.5". The bocage fronds and flowers are typical of this Group. Price B.

Figure 26.83. Lady lute player and gentleman flautist, with sheep and swan, with bocage. Attributed to Tunstall Group. H: 10.1". As in the previous example, the bocage is formed as an arc and supports the attribution. Pairs with the next example. Price B.

Figure 26.84. Body of the flautist in the previous group alongside a matching shard from the High Street, Tunstall, excavations.

Figure 26.85. Gentleman bagpiper and lady lute player, with sheep and a dog, with bocage. Attributed to Tunstall Group. H: 9.5". Pairs with the preceding example. Price B.

Figure 26.86. *VILLAGE SONGSTERS*. Lady with squirrel and gentleman bagpiper, with bocage. Attributed to Patriotic Group. H: ~9". Patriotic Group used these small tablets for titles. This is the only titled example of this group recorded. Price B.

Figure 26.87. Lady with squirrel and gentleman bagpiper, with bocage. Attributed to Patriotic Group. H: ~9". Like the previous example but the base is painted differently. Price B. *John Howard; www.antiquepottery.co.uk.*

Figure 26.88. Lady with squirrel and gentleman bagpiper, with bocage. Attributed to Patriotic Group. H: 8.9". Like the previous two examples but on an iron-red base. Price B. *John Howard; www.antiquepottery.co.uk.*

Figure 26.89. Lady with squirrel and gentleman bagpiper, with bocage. Attributed to Patriotic Group. H: ~9". Like previous examples but with yet another variation in the painting of the base. Price B.

Figure 26.90. Gentleman piper and lady with lute, with bocage. Attributed to Patriotic Group. H: ~9". An uncommon example. Also occurs on the same pink base as figure 26.86. A similar crisscross pattern is painted around the base of the dandies in figure 133.11. Price B.

Figure 26.91. *Rural Pastime.* Gentleman bagpiper and lady with dog, with bocage. Attributed to Ralph Wood; impressed "166". H: 8.7". The square base is painted with a line on only three sides, and the bocage and titling are characteristic of Ralph Wood. Price B.

Figure 26.92. *Rurel-Paftime, Rurel-Paftime*. A pair, one with gentleman bagpiper and lady with dog, the other with songstress and gentleman with tabor, with bocages. Attributed to Ralph Wood. H: 8.5". A group like that on the right is recorded marked "Ra. Wood Burslem" and another like that on the left is marked "W". Price B.

Figure 26.93. *Pastime*. Gentleman bagpiper and lady with dog, with bocage. Attributed to Ralph Wood. H: ~8.2". The more somber palette and titling suggest production later in the Ralph Wood period. Part of the bocage is original and typical. Price A.

Figure 26.94. Gentleman with tabor, with dog, with bocage. Attributed to Ralph Wood. H: ~8". The bocage and the painting of the base and mound support the attribution. From the same molds used for the hand drummer in figure 26.92.

Figure 26.95. A pair, one with lady lute player and gentleman playing horn, the other with gentleman piper and songstress, with bocages. Probably made by Enoch Wood. H: 7.8" (L), 7.5" (R). The bases and bocage fronds are typical of Enoch Wood. Price B.

Figure 26.96. Lady lute player and gentleman playing horn, with bocage. Probably made by Enoch Wood. H: 7.5". Similar to the left side of the previous pair but with a different typical Enoch Wood bocage. Price A. *Collection of Arnold and Barbara Berlin.*

Figure 26.97. Lady lute player and gentleman playing horn, with swan, with bocage. H: 9.5". With the three-leaflet bocage fronds that occur on other figures that form an as-yet unclassified Group. Companion to the next example. Price B.

Figure 26.98. Gentleman piper and lady with triangle, with swan, with bocage. H: 8.5". Companion to the previous example and has the same three-leaflet bocage fronds. Price B.

Figure 26.99. Songstress and gentleman piper, with bocage. H: 9.7". An uncommon group. The bocage is flat on the back (i.e., the fronds have not been placed back-to-back with others). Price B.

Figure 26.100. Gentleman piper and lady with dog, with bocage. Attributed to Dudson. H: ~8". The base and bocage are typical of Dudson. Price B.

Figure 26.101. Songstress and gentleman with tabor, with bocage. Attributed to Dudson. H: ~7.3". A companion subject to the previous example. Both have typical Dudson bocages with one leaflet upon seven others. Price A.

Figure 26.102. *Pastime.* Lady and gentleman with tabor, with bocage. Attributed to Dudson. H: ~8". Like the previous example but titled and with a different Dudson bocage (one leaflet atop three). Pairs with the following example. A song book may be lost from her hand. Price A.

Figure 26.103. *Pastime.* Gentleman bagpiper and lady with dog, with bocage. Attributed to Dudson. H: ~8". The base, titling, and bocage are typical of Dudson. Pairs with the preceding example. Price A.

Figure 26.104. Songstress and gentleman with tabor, with bocage. H: 7.3". Closely similar to the following examples but on a brown base. Flowers are on the bocage branches rather than on the leaves. Price A. *Elinor Penna.*

Figure 26.105. Songstress and gentleman with tabor; gentleman bagpiper and lady with sheep. A pair, with bocages. H: 7.8" (L), 7.1" (R). Price B.

Figure 26.106. *PASTIME*. Gentleman bagpiper and lady with dog, with bocage. H: 7.9". A titled example like the right hand group in the preceding pair. Its companion group would be titled *RURAL*, or *RUALERS*, or *RUALER* &. Note the large flower on the mound and the inclusion of a dog rather than the sheep previously shown. Price A.

Figure 26.107. Gentleman bagpiper and lady with dog, with bocage. H: 7.2". Distinguished by a colorfully decorated base. Two large cup-like flowers, like the flower on the previous example, are on the mound. Bocage lost. Price A. *Peter Flemans.*

Figure 26.108. *Rural*. Gentleman bagpiper and lady with dog, with bocage. H: 7.5". This titling also occurs on figure 146.33. Price B. *John Howard; www.antiquepottery.co.uk.*

Figure 26.110. *SONGSTERS*. Lady lute player and a gentleman, with dog and swan, with bocage. Impressed "WALTON". H: ~8.3". With losses. Like one of the groups in the following example but with the broad bocage leaves that Walton sometimes used. Price A.

Figure 26.109. *SONGSTERS, SONGSTERS*. A pair, one with lady lute player and gentleman horn player, the other with gentleman piper and lady with triangle, each with a swan, dog, and bocage. Both impressed "WALTON". H: 8.7". It is difficult to find a fine pair like this in good condition. Price C. *Nick Burton.*

Figure 26.111. Large pleasance with gentleman piper and lady lute player, with dog and sheep, with bocage. Attributed to "Sherratt." L: ~9.8". Examples on this base are uncommon. The bocage and its flowers are typical of "Sherratt." The musicians occur as individual figures, also attributed to "Sherratt." Price C.

Figure 26.112. Large pleasance with gentleman piper and lady lute player, with dog and sheep, with bocage. Attributed to "Sherratt." H: ~11.2". Essentially the same as the previous pleasance but on the more common "Sherratt" table base. The brown speckled painting of the bocage trunk is typical of "Sherratt." Price C.

Figure 26.113. Large pleasance with gentleman piper and lady lute player, with dog and sheep, with bocage. Attributed to "Sherratt." H: 12", L: 9.8". The floral sprigs applied to the front of the grassy mound are exclusive to "Sherratt." Price B. *Collection of Michael J. Smith.*

Figure 26.114. Small pleasance with gentleman piper and lady holding sheep, with dog and sheep, with spill vases. Attributed to "Sherratt." L: 7". The turrets are typical of "Sherratt," but their jagged upper edges are unusual. The man and lady occur within other "Sherratt" examples. Price B.

Figure 26.115. Small pleasance with gentleman piper and lady holding sheep, with dog, and sheep, with spill vases. Attributed to "Sherratt." L: 7". Similar to the previous example but decorated extensively with pink luster. "Sherratt" often decorated with pink luster. Price B.

Figure 26.116. Small pleasance with lady holding sheep, with dog and sheep, with spill vases. L: 7", H: 5". The gentleman piper once seated to the left is lost. Unusual in that two of the sheep are black, as is the trim on the turrets. Price A. *K. Gomersall.*

Figure 26.117. Gentleman bagpiper and dog, with bocage. Probably made by Enoch Wood. H: 6.2". The bocage (right side restored) and flowers are typical of Enoch Wood. With the exception of the bocage, it strongly resembles the Derby figure of circa 1765–1770. A companion lady playing the lute has been noted. Price A.

Figure 26.118. Gentleman bagpiper and dog. Possibly made by Enoch Wood. H: 6". Similar to the previous figure but made without a bocage. Price A.

Figure 26.119. Lady lute player with sheep, gentleman bagpiper with dog, a pair, with bocages. H: 7.3". Three-leaflet fronds form each bocage. After eighteenth-century Derby figures. Price B. *John Howard; www.antiquepottery.co.uk.*

Figure 26.120. Gentleman bagpiper with dog, with bocage. H: 7.1". Like the previous bagpiper but with common five-leaflet fronds for the bocage. After an eighteenth-century Derby figure. Price A. *Elinor Penna.*

Figure 26.121. Lady lute player with sheep, with bocage. H: 7.1". Like the lady with lute in figure 26.119 but with common five-leaflet bocage fronds. Pairs with the previous bagpiper. After the eighteenth-century Derby figure. Price A. *Elinor Penna.*

Figure 26.122. Flautist with music, a dog, and a book at his side, with bocage. H: 7.1". The bocage has generic five-leaflet fronds, but this figure also occurs with three-leaflet fronds. Pairs with the following lady musician, both being after eighteenth-century Derby figures. Price A. *Michael Goodacre.*

Figure 26.123. Lady lute player, with sheep and open book at her side, with bocage. H: 6.4". The bocage has five-leaflet fronds, but the figure also occurs with three-leaflet fronds. Pairs with previous flautist. Price A. *Elinor Penna.*

Figure 26.124. Lady lute player and sheep, gentleman bagpiper and dog, a pair, with bocages. H: ~6.5". Rustic derivatives of earlier porcelain figures. Price B.

Figure 26.125. Gentleman bagpiper with dog, with bocage. H: 7". Like so many similar figures, this derives from an earlier Derby figure. Price A.

Figure 26.126. Lady lute player and sheep, with bocage. H: 6.7". Price A.

Figure 26.127. Gentleman bagpiper and dog, lady lute player and sheep, a pair, with bocages. Attributed to Tunstall Group. H: 7.1" (L), 7" (R). Arc bocages occur commonly on Tunstall figures. The flowers are typical of Tunstall. The figures are derivatives of earlier Derby figures. Price B.

Figure 26.128. Gentleman bagpiper, lady lute player, reverse of previous pair.

Figure 26.129. Gentleman bagpiper and dog, with bocage. Attributed to Tunstall Group. H: 7.8". Similar to the previous bagpiper. Price A.

Figure 26.130. Gentleman bagpiper and dog, lady lute player and sheep, a pair, with bocages. Attributed to Tunstall Group. H: 7.1" (L), 7" (R). Very different from the previous Tunstall examples. The arc bocages comprise characteristic fronds and flowers. Price B.

Figure 26.131. Gentleman bagpiper and dog, lady lute player and sheep, a pair, with bocages. Attributed to Patriotic Group. H: ~6". The bocage flowers are characteristic of this Group. After Derby figures. Price B.

Figure 26.132. Lady lute player and sheep, gentleman bagpiper with dog, a pair, with bocages. Attributed to Patriotic Group. H: 5.5" (L), 5.3" (R). Similar to the previous pair but he is on a lower base. After Derby figures. Price B. *Saffron Walden Museum.*

Figure 26.133. Gentleman bagpiper and dog, with bocage. H: 6". After earlier Derby figures and, like other Staffordshire derivatives, includes a dog that closely resembles the Derby dog and is quite unlike dogs generally found on earthenware groups. Price A.

Figure 26.134. Gentleman bagpiper and dog, with bocage. H: ~6". Closely similar to the previous figure, having the same fronds but with a large flower. After the eighteenth-century Derby figure. Price A. *Phil Masters Antiques, Leek.*

Figure 26.135. Lady lute player and sheep, with bocage. H: 6". After the eighteenth-century Derby figure. Price A.

Figure 26.136. Lady lute player and sheep, with bocage. H: 6". Closely similar to the previous figure but with yellow scrolling on the base instead of blue. Price A.

Figure 26.137. Gentleman bagpiper and dog, with bocage. Attributed to Leather Leaf Group. H: 5.5". He has closed one eye and puffed out a cheek with exertion. A rustic derivative of the eighteenth-century Derby figure. The bocage flowers support the attribution. Price A.

Figure 26.138. Gentleman flautist with music, lady lute player and dog, a pair. H: 5.5" (L), 6" (R). Made without bocages. A more sophisticated portrayal. After earlier Derby figures that are also on octagonal bases. Price B.

Figure 26.139. Gentleman flautist with music. H: ~6". Made without bocage. Similar to the previous flautist but on a vermicular base. Price A.

Figure 26.140. Gentleman bugler and dog, lady lute player and dog, a pair, with bocages. Attributed to Patriotic Group. H: 6.4" (L), 6.8" (R). The bocage flowers and floral sprigs on the mounds are characteristic of the Patriotic Group, as are these bases with canted corners. Price B. *John Howard; www.antiquepottery.co.uk.*

Figure 26.141. Gentleman bugler and dog, lady lute player and dog, a pair, with bocages. Attributed to Patriotic Group. H: 7.4". These figures occur more frequently on bases with canted corners. Price B. *Brighton and Hove Museums.*

Figure 26.142. Gentleman bugler and dog, with bocage. Attributed to Patriotic Group. H: ~7". An uncommon variant of the preceding figures in that the base is painted red. Price A.

Figure 26.143. Lady with lap harp and gentleman drummer, both wearing turbans, with sheep and spill vase. Attributed to Patriotic Group. H: 7.5". The leafy sprigs applied to the base are typical of the Group. Price C.

Figure 26.144. Lady with tambourine and gentleman drummer, both wearing turbans, with spill vase. Attributed to Patriotic Group. H: 7.5". The leafy sprigs applied to the base and their distinctive flowers are characteristic of the Patriotic Group. Price C. *John Howard; www.antiquepottery.co.uk*

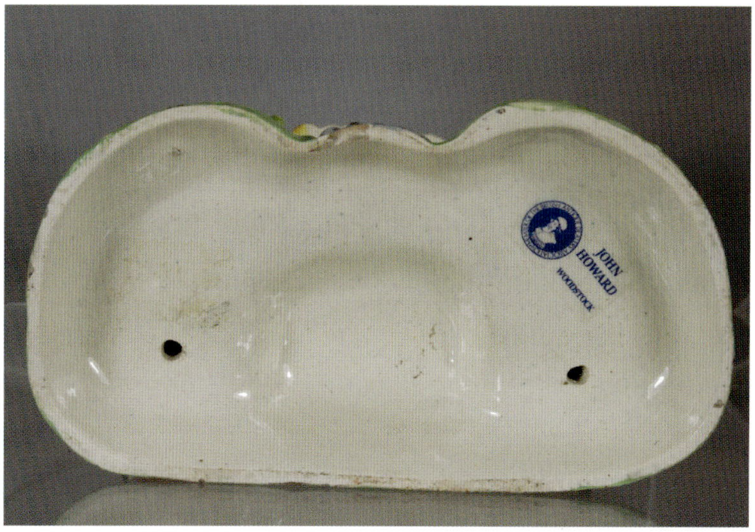

Figure 26.145. Base of previous spill vase. *John Howard; www.antiquepottery.co.uk*

Figure 26.146. Lady with tambourine and gentleman drummer, both wearing turbans, with spill vase. Attributed to Patriotic Group. H: 7.5". Like the previous examples but the vase is painted in a manner more consistent with "Sherratt". Price C.

Figure 26.147. Lady with lap harp and gentleman drummer, both wearing turbans, with sheep, shells, and spill vase. Probably attributable to Patriotic Group. H: 7.6". Similar to the previous example but with shells rather than sprigs on the base. Price C. *Collection of Michael J. Smith.*

Figure 26.148. Gentleman piper and lady lute player, with sheep and spill vase. Attributed to Patriotic Group. H: ~7.5". The sprigs on the base are typical of the Patriotic Group. Price C.

Figure 26.149. Gentleman piper and lady lute player, with sheep, shells, and spill vase. Probably attributable to Patriotic Group. H: 7.5". Similar to the preceding example but with two large shells applied to the base instead of sprigs. Price C.

Figure 26.150. Gentleman piper and lady lute player, with shells and spill vase. Probably attributable to Patriotic Group. H: 7". Closely similar to the previous two examples. The spill vase is painted in the less-common combination of yellow and blue. Price C. *Jane McClafferty.*

Figure 26.151. Lady lute player and gentleman piper, with dog, sheep, shells, and spill vase. Attributed to Leather Leaf Group. H: ~8". The musicians differ from those on previous examples, and the flowers on the base validate a Leather Leaf Group attribution. Price C.

Figure 26.152. Gentleman piper and lady lute player, with sheep, dog, shells, and spill vase. Probably attributable to Leather Leaf Group. H: 8.5". The musicians are like those in the previous example, and the spill is molded and painted similarly. Price C. *Elinor Penna.*

Figure 26.153. Gentleman flautist and lady lute player, with dog, cat, shells, and spill vase. Attributed to Patriotic Group. H: 9". The figures as well as the animals and hats strewn on the base are from the same molds that Patriotic Group used for its reading figures and its family groups. Price C.

Figure 26.154. Gentleman piper and lady lap harp player, with a sheep, dog, shells, and spill vase. Attributed to Leather Leaf Group. H: 10". This is the tallest trumpet spill vase group, and the vase is on a plinth. The figures differ from those on other spill vases. Price D.

Figure 26.155. Gentleman piper and lady lap harp player, reverse of previous example. Only one other example of this tall vase is recorded, but it instead has the piper who stands alongside the following vase.

Figure 26.156. Lady lute player and gentleman piper, with sheep, dog, shells, and spill vase. H: ~8.5". The piper differs from that on the other musical spills, but the overall composition is otherwise similar. The bottom of the vase is painted in bold stripes, as in the Leather Leaf Group examples, but this decorative feature alone cannot support attribution. Price C. *Peter Flemans.*

Figure 26.157. Drummer and piper, with dog and spill vase. Attributed to "Sherratt." H: 7". The rainbow base is specific to "Sherratt." The musicians are formed from molds used for small figures on "Sherratt" menageries. Price C.

Figure 26.158. Gentleman horn player and lady lute player, with dog and spill vase. Attributed to "Sherratt." H: 7". These musicians also occur as single "Sherratt" figures and in some "Sherratt" groups. Price C.

Figure 26.159. Lady with lap harp and gentleman piper, with sheep and spill vase. H: ~6". Note the very different trumpet spill vase. Price B. *Michael Goodacre.*

Figure 26.160. Gentleman piper and shepherdess, with dog, sheep, and goat, with candle holder and bocage. Attributed to Ralph Wood; impressed "89". H: 11". The companion group has a couple with a bird cage (Volume 3, chapter 114). Price C.

Figure 26.161. Gentleman piper and shepherdess with dog, sheep, and goat. Attributed to Ralph Wood; impressed "88" beneath. H: ~9". The body of this figure is porcelaneous. The bocage is lost. Price B. *Geoffrey Godden Collection, The Potteries Museum.*

Figure 26.162. Gentleman piper and shepherdess, with dog, sheep, and goat, with bocage. Attributed to Ralph Wood. H: 11". The bocage and rainbow palette on the base are typical of Ralph Wood. On reproductions of this group, the dog usually has its head turned to look behind it. Price B. *Halls Holdings Ltd., Shrewsbury.*

Figure 26.163. Gentleman piper and shepherdess, with dog, sheep, and goat, with bocage. Attributed to Ralph Wood. H: 10.7". Companion to figure 114.3. Price B. *Image courtesy of The Potteries Museum & Art Gallery, Stoke-on-Trent, UK.*

Figure 26.164. *Shepards.* Gentleman piper and shepherdess, with dog, sheep, and goat, with candleholder and bocage. Attributed to Ralph Wood. H: 12.2". The titling of the base and the muddier palette are characteristic of figures probably made later in the Ralph Wood period. Price B. *Dallas Auction Gallery.*

Figure 26.165. Gentleman piper and shepherdess, with sheep and goat, with bocage. H: ~11". The dog is lost from the base. Price B. *Andrew Dando Antiques.*

Figure 26.166. *Shepherd.* Gentleman piper and shepherdess, with dog, goat, and sheep, with bocage. Attributed to Dudson. H: ~12.5". The bocage and base, including the titling, are typical of Dudson. A companion *Bird-catchers* group is in Volume 3, figure 114.5. Price C. *John Howard; www.antiquepottery.co.uk.*

Figure 26.167. Gentleman piper, lady with tambourine, a pair. She is impressed "NEALE & Co"; he is unmarked but attributed to Neale. H: 8". Both are decorated in a typical Neale palette, and the glazes are particularly fine and silky to the touch. Made without bocages. Price C.

Figure 26.168. Gentleman piper, lady with tambourine, reverse of previous pair.

Figure 26.169. Gentleman piper. Impressed "NEALE & Co". H: 8". Like the unmarked piper of the preceding pair. The base style and the superior glaze and enameling are typical of Neale. Made without bocage. Price B.

Figure 26.170. *Flemifh Music, Flemifh Music*. Lady lute player, gentleman with hurdy-gurdy, a pair. Impressed "Ra. Wood Burslem". H: 8.9" (L), 9.4" (R). The pair display typical Ralph Wood features, including the color palette, the bases, and the script used for the titles. Price C.

Figure 26.171. *Flemifh Music, Flemifh Music,* bases of previous pair showing the impressed "Ra. Wood Burslem" mark on each.

Figure 26.172. *Flemifh Music, Flemifh Music*. Lady lute player, gentleman with hurdy-gurdy, a pair. Attributed to Ralph Wood. Both impressed "132". H: 8.8" (L). 9.2" (R). Similar to the preceding pair and with impressed numbers associated with Ralph Wood. Price B.

Figure 26.173. *Flemifh Music, Flemifh Music*, previous pair with "132" impressed on the back of each base.

Figure 26.174. *Flemifh Music, Flemifh Music*. Gentleman with hurdy-gurdy, lady lute player, a pair. Attributed to Ralph Wood. He impressed "132"; she impressed "131". H: ~9.2" (L), 8.8" (R). Price B. *John Howard; www.antiquepottery.co.uk.*

Figure 26.175. *Flemish Music, & Partner*. Gentleman with hurdy-gurdy, lady lute player, a pair. Attributed to Ralph Wood. H: 9.4" (L), 8.5" (R). Unmarked, but close similarities to the preceding examples support the attribution, despite the slight modification in titles. Price B. *Brighton and Hove Museums.*

Figure 26.176. Gentleman with hurdy-gurdy. H: 8.3". Finely made with no features to establish an attribution. Price A. *Andrew Dando Antiques.*

Figure 26.177. Gentleman with hurdy-gurdy. Impressed "Enoch Wood & ..."(illegible). H: 7.4". Very similar to the male *Flemifh Music* by Ralph Wood, but the mode of decoration is quite different and the figure is more wooden. Price A.

Figure 26.178. Lady lute player. Possibly made by Enoch Wood. H: ~7". Companion to the preceding figure. Price A.

Figure 26.179. Gentleman with hurdy-gurdy. Possibly made by Enoch Wood. H: 9". Very similar to the preceding marked Enoch Wood figure on a mound, and the base is a typical Enoch Wood base. Price A. *Brighton and Hove Museums.*

Figure 26.180. Lady lute player. Possibly made by Enoch Wood. H: ~8.4". Companion to the preceding hurdy-gurdy player. Price A.

Figure 26.181. Gentleman with hurdy-gurdy, lady lute player, a pair. Possibly made by Enoch Wood. H: ~9" (L), 8.4" (R). Similarities in painting suggest that these figures are an original pairing. Most pairs today are assembled from odd single figures. Price B. *Andrew Dando Antiques.*

Figure 26.182. Gentleman with hurdy-gurdy. H: 9". Closely similar to previous hurdy-gurdy players but painted in an unusual style. Price A. *Michael Grana.*

Figure 26.183. Gentleman with hurdy-gurdy. H: 8.4". From different molds to previous examples. His face is broader, the modeling of the clothes differs, and the hurdy-gurdy's sound hole is pierced rather than merely painted. Price A.

Figure 26.184. Gentleman with hurdy-gurdy atop a plinth with a classical motif. H: 10.5". Painted "15" on the reverse of the plinth. Pairs with the following lady with lute. Classical personifications of the seasons occur on similar plinths (figs. 155.108–113). Price B, pair. *Andrew Dando Antiques.*

Figure 26.185. Lady lute player atop a plinth with a classical motif. H: 10.5". Painted "13" on the back of the plinth. Pairs with the previous hurdy-gurdy player. Price B, pair. *Andrew Dando Antiques.*

Figure 26.186. Lady lute player and gentleman hurdy-gurdy player, reverse of previous two figures showing "13" and "15" painted on the plinths. A classical motif is on only the front of each plinth. *Andrew Dando Antiques.*

Figure 26.187. *Flemish Music.* Gentleman with hurdy-gurdy. Attributed to Dudson. H: ~7.5". Pairs with the following *Mate.* Both figures appear to come from Ralph Wood molds but large cloaks have been added. The glazes, bases, and titling are typical of Dudson, and such cloaks are only recorded on Dudson figures. Price B, pair. *Andrew Dando Antiques.*

Figure 26.188. *Mate.* Lady with lute. Attributed to Dudson. H: ~7.5". Pairs with the previous figure. Price B, pair. *Andrew Dando Antiques.*

Figure 26.189. *Flemish Music, Mate*. Reverse of previous two figures. *Andrew Dando Antiques.*

Figure 26.190. *Gasconian, Mate*. Gentleman musician, lady carrying pitchers, a pair. Attributed to Dudson. H: ~8" (L), 10" (R). Mate shown at reduced size. After Ralph Wood's *Gasconian* and figure of a water carrier. The titling is typical of Dudson and such cloaks are known only on Dudson figures. Price B. *Andrew Dando Antiques.*

Figure 26.191. *A Gafconian.* Gentleman musician. Attributed to Ralph Wood; impressed "66". H: 8". This figure also occurs impressed "65", "67", "68", and "99" (probably intended to be "66"). Impressed numbers on Ralph Wood figures usually vary within a close range. Price B. *Mary and Maurice Norton.*

Figure 26.192. *Gasconian.* Gentleman musician. Attributed to Ralph Wood; impressed "65". H: 8". The title differs slightly from that of the previous example. Price B. *Brighton and Hove Museums.*

Figure 26.193. Gasconian, gentleman musician. Attributed to Ralph Wood; impressed "66". Ralph Wood figures sometimes occur on unpainted square bases. Price B. *Aurea Carter Antiques.*

Figure 26.194. *Spanifh Dancer, Spanifh Dancer.* Gentleman with castanets, lady with hand drum, a pair. Attributed to Ralph Wood; impressed "71"(L), "73"(R). H: 8.3" (L), 7.8" (R). The female figure is also recorded impressed "72". Price B.

Figure 26.195. *Spanifh Dancer, Spanifh Dancer,* reverse of previous pair showing an impressed number on the back of each base.

Figure 26.196. *Bag Piper*. Gentleman bagpiper. Attributed to Ralph Wood; impressed "21". H: 8.3". Made without a bocage. Price A.

Figure 26.197. Gentleman bagpiper, with bocage. Attributed to Dudson. H: ~8". The figure appears to have been formed from Ralph Wood molds, but the bocage fronds and the x-sprigs on the base are specific to Dudson. Price A.

Figure 26.198. Gentleman bagpiper, with bocage. Attributed to Dudson. H: ~8". Price A. *Andrew Dando Antiques.*

Figure 26.199. Gentleman piper, reverse of previous example. *Andrew Dando Antiques.*

Figure 26.200. Gentleman horn player. Possibly made by Enoch Wood. H: 9.2". The base is typical of Enoch Wood. Price A. *Aurea Carter Antiques.*

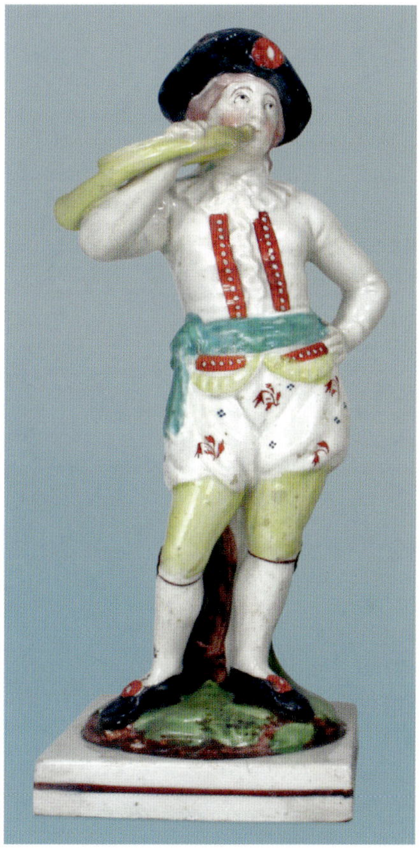

Figure 26.201. Gentleman horn player. Possibly made by Enoch Wood. H: ~9.2". Like the preceding figure but decorated differently. Price A.

Figure 26.202. Lady with tambourine. Possibly made by Enoch Wood. H: 8.8". Pairs with a horn player of the type in the previous two examples. Price A.

Figure 26.203. Gentleman piper. H: 8.3". A rare figure that presumably pairs with a female partner. Price A.

Figure 26.204. Gentleman piper leaning against a rock, with dog and sheep, with bocage. Attributed to "Sherratt." H: 7.1". The double-lined base and the bocage (oak-leaf fronds with mayflowers) are typical of Sherratt. Price B.

Figure 26.205. Gentleman piper leaning against a rock, with dog and sheep, with bocage. Attributed to "Sherratt." H: ~7.1". Like the previous example but with fern bocage fronds. A perky dog of this form is frequently on "Sherratt" groups. Price B. *Andrew Dando Antiques.*

Figure 26.206. Gentleman piper with sheep. Attributed to Ralph Wood. H: 8", L: 7". The line is painted on three sides of the base, and the figure is from the same molds as the following piper. Made without bocage. Price A. *G. Lyle Richardson.*

Figure 26.207. Gentleman piper with sheep, with bocage. Attributed to Ralph Wood. H: ~8". The rainbow colors on the mound and the bocage are typical of Ralph Wood. Price A.

Figure 26.208. Lady mandolin player, gentleman with triangle, and gentleman flautist, with swans, with bocage. Probably made by Dale. H: ~8.5". Rare. Groups of three musicians are uncommon. These twelve-petalled bocage flowers occur only on Dale and Tittensor figures. The triangle player's head is restored. The other musicians have typical Dale faces. Price B.

Figure 26.209. Lady tambourine player, gentleman horn player, and gentleman drummer, with dog and bocage. Attributed to Patriotic Group. H: 8.1". A rare group. The turbaned musicians also appear on Patriotic Group trumpet spill vases, and the large flowers on the arc bocage are characteristic of the Patriotic Group. Price D.

Figure 26.210. Gentleman drummer and lady tambourine player in an arbor. H: 6". A rare group. Price D.

Figure 26.211. Gentleman bugler, lady tambourine player, a pair, with bocages. Attributed to Dale. H: 7.8" (L), 7.1" (R). This is the tallest pair of Dale musicians. The flowers and the figures' faces are typical of Dale. A rare pair. Price B.

Figure 26.212. Lady tambourine player, gentleman bugler, a pair, with bocages. Impressed "WALTON". H: 6"(L), 6.2" (R). An attractive and rather uncommon pair. Price B. *Brighton and Hove Museums (L), Michael Goodacre (R).*

Figure 26.213. Gentleman bugler, lady tambourine player, a pair with bocages. H: 5.6" (L), 6.3" (R). Price A.

Figure 26.214. Lady tambourine player, with bocage. Impressed "SALT". H: ~6". Price A.

Figure 26.215. *SHOW MAN* (faintly impressed). Gentleman bugler, with bocage. Possibly made by Salt. H: ~6". Close similarities to the previous tambourine player (impressed "SALT") suggest a Salt attribution. Price A.

Figure 26.216. Gentleman bugler, lady tambourine player, a pair, with bocages. H: 5.8" (L), 5.9" (R). Both figures have Salt-like features, but marked Salt figures never have blue bocage flowers and the fan-like molding seen on the lower front edges of these bases. Price A.

Figure 26.217. Gentleman bugler, with bocage. H: ~6". With Salt-like features that are insufficient for attribution. Price A. *Martyn Edgell Antiques Ltd.*

Figure 26.218. *SHOW M* (title partially impressed). H: 5.1". Price A. *Michael Goodacre.*

Figure 26.219. Gentleman bugler, lady tambourine player, a pair, with bocages. H: ~6.3". These are somewhat larger figures. Despite their Salt-like features, examples are never marked and are unlikely to have been made by Salt. Price A.

Figure 26.220. *SHOW WOMAN* and *SHOW MAN*. Lady tambourine player, gentleman bugler, a pair with bocages. Attributed to Patriotic Group. H: 5.9". This pair has characteristic Patriotic bocage flowers. Price B.

Figure 26.221. *SHOW MAN* and *SHOW WOMAN* (faintly impressed). Gentleman bugler, lady tambourine player, a pair, with bocages. Attributed to Patriotic Group. H: ~5.9". Similar to the previous pair but with the titles painted over in green. Price B. *John Howard; www.antiquepottery.co.uk.*

Figure 26.222. Gentleman bugler, lady tambourine player, a pair, with bocages. Attributed to Tunstall Group. H: ~5.5". The flowers are typical of Tunstall. Price B.

Figure 26.223. A matching shard from the High Street, Tunstall, excavations.

Figure 26.224. Gentleman bugler, lady tambourine player, a pair, with bocages. Attributed to Tunstall Group. H: 6" (L), 5.4" (R). Differs markedly from the previous Tunstall pair, but with typical Tunstall flowers. This base is specific to Tunstall. The size variation is probably caused by differences in firing. Price A.

Figure 26.225. *SHOW WOMAN* (faintly impressed). Lady tambourine player, with bocage. Attributed to Daisy Group. H: ~5.5". Price A.

Figure 26.226. Gentleman bugler, with bocage. Probably made by Enoch Wood. H: 5.6". The bocage and base with "16" impressed beneath are typical of Enoch Wood. A companion bocage figure has not been recorded. Price A.

Figure 26.227. Gentleman bugler. Possibly made by Enoch Wood. H: ~5.2". Made without bocage. Made from many of the same figure molds as used for the previous example. Companion to the following tambourine player. Price A. *Andrew Dando Antiques.*

Figure 26.228. Lady tambourine player. Possibly made by Enoch Wood. H: 4.9". Made without bocage. The thick-walled base with an impressed "30" and painted "5" beneath is typical of Enoch Wood. Price A.

Figure 26.229. Lady tambourine player, with bocage. H: 4.9". Her companion is not recorded. This colorful base occurs on other figures. Several pot banks used this bocage on smaller figures. Some restoration to tambourine. Price A.

Figure 26.230. Gentleman horn player with dog, with bocage. H: ~6.3". The Salt-like bocage is insufficient basis for attribution. Price A.

Figure 26.231. Gentleman horn player, with bocage. H: 6.3". From the same molds as the previous figure. Price A. *Andrew Dando Antiques.*

Figure 26.232. Lady tambourine player. Probably made by the Scottish east coast potteries. H: 5.2". The color palette (with mostly under-glaze colors and some enamels) is typical of the Scottish potteries. Price A. *Peter Flemans.*

Figure 26.233. Lady lute player and gentleman horn player, gentleman piper and lady with triangle, each couple with a dog and swan, with bocage. H: 12". Known as a "double songsters group" because the figures are from the molds used for the figures in the two Walton groups titled *SONGSTERS* (fig. 26.109). There is no basis for attributing this large group to Walton. Price C. *John Howard; www.antiquepottery.co.uk.*

Figure 26.234. Lady lute player and gentleman horn player, gentleman piper and lady with triangle, each couple with a dog and swan, with spill vase. H: ~11". Very like the previous example but with a spill vase in place of the bocage. Price C. *Eileen and Robert Carde.*

Figure 26.235. Lady lute player and gentleman horn player, gentleman piper and lady with triangle, each couple with a swan, with bocage. H: 10.4". Note the blue-sponged base with canted corners and the large bocage. Price C.

Figure 26.236. Lady lute player and gentleman horn player, gentleman piper and lady with sticks, each couple with a swan, with spill vase. H: 9.5". Unlike previous examples, the lady holds sticks rather than a triangle. Also, the structure supporting the vase sits lower, suggesting that some other pot bank made this group. Price C.

Work

27. Shepherds and Shepherdesses

A multitude of early Staffordshire figures incorporate small sheep, but the figures shown here portray the shepherd most usually with his dog and the shepherdess with her lamb. As pairs, these figures are sometimes titled *SHEPHERD* and *SHEPHERDESS*, or *BOY AND DOG* and *GIRL AND LAMB*. Other examples of people and dogs are shown elsewhere, as are shepherd musicians (chapter 26).

Figure 27.1. Boy with dog, with bocage. Possibly made by Enoch Wood. H: 5". The ochre line around the base, the formation of the base, and the flowers on the mound suggest the attribution. Companion subject to the following figure. Price A.

Figure 27.2. Girl with lamb, with bocage. Possibly made by Enoch Wood. H: 4.8". The base and the flowers on the mound are suggestive of Enoch Wood. Companion subject to the previous figure. Price A. *Brighton and Hove Museums.*

Figure 27.3. Boy with dog, girl with lamb, a pair, with bocages. Attributed to Dudson. H: ~5". The bocages support the attribution. Dudson commonly painted bases brown, but these bases are unusual in that only the tops are painted. Price A.

Figure 27.4. Girl with lamb, with bocage. H: ~5". The bocage differs from that on other similar figures shown here, suggesting that this figure was made by yet another pot bank. Price A.

Figure 27.5. Girl with lamb, with bocage. H: ~5". These three-leaflet bocage fronds occur on an unclassified Group of figures. Companion to the following figure. Price A.

Figure 27.6. Boy with dog, with bocage. H: ~5". Companion to the previous figure, both having three-leaflet bocage fronds. Price A.

Figure 27.7. Boy with dog, with bocage. H: ~5". From the same molds as the previous figure. This bocage is unusual, but both figures may be from the same pot bank. Price A.

Figure 27.8. Detail of the bocage on the previous figure. The tip of each frond is curled and painted red.

Figure 27.9. Boy with dog, with bocage. H: ~5". Price A.

Figure 27.10. Girl with lamb, with bocage. Impressed "WALTON". H: 5.7". Price A.

Figure 27.11. Girl with lamb, with bocage. Impressed "WALTON". H: 5.8". Like the previous figure, but differences in the painting and positioning of the head alter her appearance. Companion subject to the Walton boy with dog in the following examples. Price A.

Figure 27.12. Boy with dog, with bocage. Impressed "WALTON". H: ~5.5". A companion subject to the previous Walton girl-and-lamb figures. Price A.

Figure 27.13. Boy with dog, with bocage. Impressed "WALTON". H: ~5.5". The base differs from that of the previous figure. Price A.

Figure 27.14. Boy with dog, with bocage. Possibly made by Walton. H: ~5.5". Although unmarked, the figure is very like marked Walton versions. Price A.

Figure 27.15. Girl with lamb, with bocage. H: 7.2". The companion figure is unrecorded. Price B.

Figure 27.16. *BOY AND DOG*, with bocage. H: ~6". Attributed to Blue Group. The bocage supports the attribution. Price A.

Figure 27.17. Boy with dog, with bocage. Attributed to "Sherratt." H: ~5". The tiny flowers on the bocage are typical of "Sherratt" but are more commonly placed elsewhere on figures. The base supports the attribution. Price A.

Figure 27.18. Boy with dog, with bocage. Attributed to Edge & Grocott. H: ~5.5". A mark is poorly impressed on a ribbon behind the figure. The shape of the ribbon and the shape of the base are consistent with the attribution. The bocage is restored. Price A.

Figure 27.19. *GIRL AND LAMB*, with bocage. Impressed "SALT". H: 5.7". Companion to the titled Salt *BOY AND DOG* on the same base (fig. 27.22). Price A. *William Brook.*

Figure 27.20. *GIRL AND LAMB*, with bocage. Impressed "SALT". H: 5.5". Price A. *Woolley and Wallis Salisbury Salerooms Ltd.*

Figure 27.21. *GIRL AND LAMB* (title faintly impressed), with bocage. Impressed "SALT". H: ~5.7". Bocage restored. Price A.

Figure 27.22. *BOY AND DOG,* with bocage. Impressed "SALT". H: 5.5". Companion to the titled Salt *GIRL AND LAMB* on the same base (fig. 27.19). Price A. *Mary and Maurice Norton.*

Figure 27.23. Boy with dog, with bocage. H: ~5.8". A Salt-type bocage but probably not made by Salt because blue carnations are not recorded on marked Salt figures. Price A.

Figure 27.24. Boy with dog, with bocage. H: ~5.8". Like the previous figure, but flowers are also on the back of the bocage. Price A.

Figure 27.25. BOY A D DOG. Impressed "HALL". H: 6.3". The bocage with oak leaves and red acorns is characteristic of Hall. Price A. *Bearnes Hampton & Littlewood.*

Figure 27.26. Detail of the Hall mark impressed into the body of the previous figure. *Bearnes Hampton & Littlewood.*

Figure 27.27. Girl with lamb, with bocage. Attributed to Enoch Wood. H: ~5.5". Like the following figure but with a different bocage. Price A.

Figure 27.28. Detail of the hawthorn leaf bocage fronds on the previous example.

Figure 27.29. Girl with lamb. Attributed to Enoch Wood. H: 5.3". Both the base and bocage match excavated examples from the Burslem Old Town Hall site. Companion to the following figure, both having fern-leaflet bocage fronds. Price A. *Andrew Dando Antiques.*

Figure 27.30. Boy with dog, with bocage. Attributed to Enoch Wood. H: ~5.5". Companion to the previous girl with lamb. Matches the following excavated figure. Price A.

Figure 27.31. Boy with dog, excavated from the Burslem Old Town Hall site associated with Enoch Wood. *Image courtesy of The Potteries Museum & Art Gallery, Stoke-on-Trent, UK.*

Figure 27.32. Girl with lamb, with bocage. H: ~5.2". Price A.

Figure 27.33. *ROM AND DOG.* Boy with dog, with bocage. H: ~6". Price A.

Figure 27.34. Boy with dog, with bocage. Attributed to Dale. H: ~5.8". The grape sprig on the base confirms the attribution. Price A.

Figure 27.35. Boy with dog, with bocage. Attributed to Dale. H: 5.3". From the same molds as the previous figure. The floral sprig and indented comb marks support the attribution. Partial loss of bocage. Price A.

Figure 27.36. Detail of previous example showing the combed indentations and the floral sprig on the base.

Figure 27.37. Girl with lamb, with bocage. Attributed to Dale. H: ~6". The flowers are a strong indicator of a Dale attribution. The bocage leaves are typical of Dale. Price A.

Figure 27.38. *GIRL AND LAMB,* with bocage. Attributed to Daisy Group. H: ~5.8". Price A.

Figure 27.39. *BOY AND DOG,* with bocage. Attributed to Patriotic Group. H: 5.2". The bocage flowers establish the attribution. The companion figure follows. Price A. *Michael Goodacre.*

Figure 27.40. *GIRL AND LAMB,* with bocage. Attributed to Patriotic Group. H: 5.2". Pairs with the previous figure, but the bocage is restored. Price A. *Michael Goodacre.*

Figure 27.41. *SHEPERD, SHEPERDISS.* Shepherd with dog, shepherdess with lamb, a pair, with bocages. She is impressed "HALL"; he is unmarked but attributed to Hall. H: ~6". Hall favored a combination of red and blue carnations. Price B.

Figure 27.42. Shepherd with dog, shepherdess with lamb, with bocages. Both impressed "WALTON". H: 5.6". The shepherd differs from the following Walton shepherds. Price B. *Andrew Dando Antiques.*

Figure 27.43. Shepherdess with lamb, with bocage. Impressed "WALTON". H: ~5.6". Possibly from some of the same molds as the previous shepherdess but on a different base. Price A.

Figure 27.44. Shepherd with dog, with bocage. Impressed "WALTON". H: ~5.7". Quite different from the Walton shepherd in figure 27.42. Price A.

Figure 27.45. Shepherd with dog, with bocage. Impressed "WALTON". H: 5.5". Like the previous shepherd but with an anthemion bocage, as occurs only occasionally on Walton figures. Price A.

Figure 27.46. Shepherd with dog, with bocage. H: ~5.7". Unmarked and indistinguishable in form from marked Walton examples, but the brown base is atypical of Walton. Price A.

Figure 27.47. Shepherd with dog, with bocage. H: ~5.9". Unusual in that the dog is tucked beneath his arm. Price A.

Figure 27.48. Shepherd with dog, shepherdess with lamb, a pair, with bocages. Attributed to Patriotic Group. H: ~5.5". Pinecone bocages are specific to this Group. Price B.

Figure 27.49. *SHEPERD, SHEPERDESS.* A pair, he with dog, she with sheep, with bocages. Attributed to Patriotic Group. H: 5.5". The bocage flowers are specific to the Patriotic Group. Price B. *John Howard; www.antiquepottery.co.uk.*

Figure 27.50. Shepherd with dog, with bocage. Attributed to Patriotic Group. H: ~5". With the same distinctive bocage flowers as the previous shepherd. Price A.

Figure 27.51. *SH...SS, SHE...RD* (faintly impressed). Shepherdess with lamb, shepherd with dog, a pair, with bocages. Attributed to Daisy Group. H: ~5.5". The shepherd, like many others, holds a small book or song sheet in his hand. Price B.

Figure 27.52. Shepherd with dog, shepherdess with lambs, an assembled pair, with bocages. Attributed to "Sherratt." H: ~6". Both have typical Sherratt bases and bocages. The shepherdess is known only from this example. Price B.

Figure 27.53. *SHEPHERD.* Shepherd with dog, with bocage. Attributed to "Sherratt." H: ~6.2". Like the previous shepherd but titled. Price A.

Figure 27.54. *SHEPHERD.* Shepherd with dog, with bocage. Attributed to "Sherratt." H: ~6.2.". Like previous "Sherratt" shepherds but with different bocage flowers. Price A.

Figure 27.55. Shepherd with dog, with bocage. Attributed to "Sherratt." H: ~6.3". From the same molds as previous similar figures but with a different base and pose. Bocage restored. Price A.

Figure 27.56. Shepherd, with bocage. Attributed to "Sherratt." H: ~6.3". On the same base as the previous example but painted differently. The figure was made without a dog. Bocage restored. Price A.

Figure 27.57. Shepherdess with lamb, with bocage. H: ~6". Attributed to "Sherratt." Price A.

Figure 27.58. Shepherdess with lamb, with bocage. Attributed to "Sherratt." H: ~6.2". Like the previous shepherdess but with different bocage flowers. Price A.

Figure 27.59. Shepherd with dog, shepherdess with lamb, a pair, with bocages. Attributed to "Sherratt." H: 6". The bocage fronds, the flowers, the dog, and the dress pattern support the attribution. These figures also occur titled *SHEPERD* and *SHEPERDISS*. Price B.

Figure 27.60. *SHEPERD*. Shepherd, with bocage. Attributed to "Sherratt." H: 6.2". Like the previous shepherd. The bocage flowers are typical of "Sherratt." Note the moustache, which has been observed on another similar "Sherratt" shepherd. Price A.

Figure 27.61. Shepherd with dog, with bocage. Attributed to Edge & Grocott. H: ~5.8". A mark is poorly impressed on a ribbon behind the figure. The shape of the ribbon and the shape of the base are consistent with the attribution. The bocage is restored. Price A.

Figure 27.62. Shepherd with dog and holding another dog, shepherdess with lamb, a pair, with bocages. Attributed to Tunstall Group. H: ~5.4". Price A.

Figure 27.63. Shepherd with dog, with bocage. Attributed to Tunstall Group. H: ~5.9". The bocage flowers are characteristic, and other "Tunstall" figures also have bocage leaves painted in this manner. Price A.

Figure 27.64. Shepherd holding a dog, with bocage. Attributed to Tunstall Group. H: ~5.7". A companion to the following shepherdess. Price A.

Figure 27.65. Shepherdess with lamb, with bocage. Attributed to Tunstall Group. H: ~5.7". A companion to the previous shepherd. Price A.

Figure 27.66. *SHEPHERDESS*. Shepherdess with lamb, with bocage. Impressed "I. DALE BURSLEM". H: ~6". These eight-petalled bocage flowers and her plump facial features are typical of Dale figures. Price B.

Figure 27.67. *SHEPHERD*. Shepherd with dog, with bocage. Impressed "I. DALE BURSLEM". H: 6". Pairs with the previous shepherdess and is titled similarly. Restoration to left side of bocage. Price B.

Figure 27.68. Reverse of previous example with John Dale's mark impressed in a curve.

Figure 27.69. Shepherd with dog, with bocage. Attributed to Dale. H: ~5.6". Like the previous shepherd made by Dale. Pairs with the following shepherdess and has the same base and bocage. Price A.

Figure 27.70. Shepherdess with lamb, with bocage. Attributed to Dale. H: ~5.6". From the same figure molds as the previous titled shepherdess made by Dale. Companion to the previous shepherd. The scrolling and apple-green enameling on the base occur on other Dale figures. Price A.

Figure 27.71. *SHEPERD.* Shepherd with dog, with bocage. H: ~5.9". Price A.

Figure 27.72. Shepherd with dog, with bocage. Attributed to Straw Flower Group. H: ~5.5". There are straw flowers on the base, and the five-petalled bocage flowers have clefts in the petals. Price A.

Figure 27.73. Shepherdess with lamb, with bocage. H: ~5.5". The bocage flowers are like those on the following shepherd, but painted differently. Price A.

Figure 27.74. Shepherd with dog, with bocage. H: ~5.5". From the same figure molds and with the same unusual base as the following shepherd. Left side of bocage restored. Price A.

Figure 27.75. Shepherd with dog, with bocage. H: ~5.5". The base is from the same molds as the base of the previous shepherd. The bocage, the figure, and the dog are as in figure 27.72, attributed to the Straw Flower Group. Price A. *Peter Flemans.*

Figure 27.76. *SHEP…IS* (title partially impressed). Shepherdess with lamb, with bocage. H: ~5.8". Unmarked but with Salt-type features. Price A.

Figure 27.77. *SHEPERDISS.* Shepherdess with lamb, with bocage. Impressed "SALT". H: ~5.8". Price A.

Figure 27.78. Shepherd with bocage. Impressed "SALT". H: ~5.8". Similar marked examples occur with a small dog on the left, and the dog may be lost from this figure. Price A.

Figure 27.79. Shepherd with dog, with bocage. Impressed "SALT". H: ~6". Price A.

Figure 27.80. Shepherd with dog, with bocage. H: ~5.8". Very like the previous Salt figures, but there are flowers on both the front and back of the bocage. Price A.

Figure 27.81. Shepherd with dog, with bocage. H: ~5.8". Like previous Salt and Salt-type figures. Unusual in that all the carnations on the bocage are blue. Blue carnations are not recorded on marked Salt figures. Price A.

Figure 27.82. Shepherd with dog, shepherdess with lamb, a pair, with bocages. H: ~5.8". Price A.

Figure 27.83. *SHEPERD, SHEPERDESS.* Shepherd with dog, shepherdess with lamb, a pair, with bocages. Probably attributable to Box Title Group. H: ~5.8". Price A.

Figure 27.84. *SHEPERD.* Shepherd with dog, with bocage. Attributed to Box Title Group. H: 5.5". Pairs with the following shepherdess. Price A. *Cynthia Bell Wolodkin, Golden Retriever Antiques.*

Figure 27.85. *SHEPERDESS.* Shepherdess with lamb, with bocage. Attributed to Box Title Group. H: 5.5". Pairs with the previous shepherd. Price A.

Figure 27.86. *SHEPERDISS.* Shepherdess with lamb, with bocage. Attributed to Box Title Group. H: ~5.5". Turquoise and green bases occur on other Box Title examples. Price A.

Figure 27.87. Shepherd with dog, with bocage. Attributed to Blue Group. H: ~5.8". Companion to the following shepherdess. Price A.

Figure 27.88. Shepherdess with lamb, with bocage. H: ~5.8". Probably attributable to Blue Group. The bocage is restored. Companion to previous shepherd. Price A.

Figure 27.89. Shepherd with dog, with bocage. Made by Enoch Wood. Excavated from the Burslem Old Town Hall site associated with Enoch Wood. H: 4.5". *Image courtesy of The Potteries Museum & Art Gallery, Stoke-on-Trent, UK.*

Figure 27.90. Shepherd with dog, with bocage. Attributed to Enoch Wood. H: ~4.7". Matches the previous figure excavated from the Burslem Old Town Hall site. Price A.

Figure 27.91. Shepherdess with lamb, with bocage. Made by Enoch Wood. Excavated from the Burslem Old Town Hall site associated with Enoch Wood; impressed "15". H: 4.5". *Image courtesy of The Potteries Museum & Art Gallery, Stoke-on-Trent, UK.*

Figure 27.92. Shepherdess with lamb, with bocage. Attributed to Enoch Wood. H: ~4.7". Matches the shepherdess excavated from the Burslem Old Town Hall site. Price A.

Figure 27.93. Shepherd with dog, shepherdess with lamb, a pair, with bocages. Probably made by Enoch Wood. H: ~4.7". Like the previous Enoch Wood figures but with different typical Enoch Wood bocages. Price B.

Figure 27.94. Shepherdess with lamb, with bocage. H: ~4.7". Price A.

Figure 27.95. *SHEPERD*. Shepherd with dog, with bocage. H: ~4.8". This bocage occurs on unclassified figures probably from a common pot bank (see Volume 2, fig. 108.36). Price A.

Figure 27.96. Shepherd with dog, with bocage. H: ~4.5". Pairs with the following shepherdess. Price A.

Figure 27.97. Shepherdess with lamb, with bocage. H: 4.5". Pairs with the previous figure. Several pot banks made hawthorn bocages of this form. Price A. *Brighton & Hove Museums.*

Figure 27.98. Shepherdess with lamb, with bocage. H: ~4.8". Price A.

Figure 27.99. Shepherdess with lamb, with bocage. H: ~4.8". Price A.

Figure 27.100. Shepherdess with lamb, with bocage. H: ~4.8". Note the bocage leaf on the lamb's back. Price A.

Figure 27.101. Shepherd with dog, shepherdess with lamb, a pair, with bocages. H: ~4.8". The lamb has a bocage leaf on its back, as in the previous example, and these figures may have a common source. Price A.

Figure 27.102. Shepherd with dog, shepherdess with lamb, a pair, with bocages. H: ~5". These three-leaflet bocage fronds occur on a group of figures that await classification. Price A.

Figure 27.103. Shepherd with dog, shepherdess with lamb, a pair, with bocages. H: ~5". Like the previous pair but his hat is different and the bases have been cut out. Price A.

Figure 27.104. Shepherdess with lamb, with bocage. H: ~5". From the same figure and base molds as the previous two shepherdesses but with differences in the bocage and decoration. Price A.

Figure 27.105. Shepherd with dog, with bocage. H: ~4.5". Price A.

Figure 27.106. Shepherdess seated with sheep, with bocage. Attributed to "Sherratt." H: 4.2". The floral sprigs on the base are characteristic of "Sherratt," and the bocage and dress pattern are typical. Companion to figure 26.17. Price B.

Figure 27.107. Shepherdess seated with sheep, with bocage. Possibly attributable to "Sherratt." H: ~4". Like the previous figure but lacks definitive features for an attribution. Price A. *Woolley and Wallis Salisbury Salerooms Ltd.*

Figure 27.108. Shepherd slumbering, with dog. L: ~6". Made without bocage. Price B.

Figure 27.109. Shepherd slumbering, with dog, with bocage. Attributed to "Sherratt." L: ~6". The bocage (with some restoration), base, and floral sprigs on the base confirm the attribution. Note the luster scrolls on the base. Pairs with the following figure. Price B.

Figure 27.110. Shepherdess slumbering, with sheep, with bocage. Probably made by "Sherratt." L: ~6". The bocage and base (both formerly lost) have been restored so that this figure pairs with the previous shepherd. Price A.

Figure 27.111. Shepherd with dog and lamb, with bocage. Attributed to Ralph Wood. H: ~6". A typical Ralph Wood base and bocage (with some restoration). A very similar example impressed "W" on the back of the base and with a good, unrestored Ralph Wood bocage is recorded. Price A.

Figure 27.112. Shepherd with lamb, with bocage. Attributed to Ralph Wood. H: ~6". A typical Ralph Wood bocage. This muddier palette usually occurs on Ralph Wood figures that are frequently titled in large, dark script. The dog is possibly lost. Price A.

Figure 27.113. Shepherd with dog and lamb, with bocage. Attributed to Dudson. H: ~6". The bocage supports the attribution. Companion to the following shepherdess. Price A.

Figure 27.114. Shepherdess with dog, with bocage. Attributed to Dudson. H: ~6". Companion to the previous shepherd. Price A.

Figure 27.115. Shepherd with lambs, with bocage. H: ~5.5". Price A.

Figure 27.116. Shepherd with shepherdess holding lamb, with bocage. H: 8.5". Pairs with the following group. Price B. *John Howard; www.antiquepottery.co.uk.*

Figure 27.117. Shepherd and shepherdess, with dog, goat, and sheep, with bocage. H: 9.5". Pairs with the previous group. Price B. *John Howard; www.antiquepottery.co.uk.*

Figure 27.118. Shepherd and shepherdess, reverse of previous example. Each bocage leaf is flat on the back because the leaves have not been paired back-to-back with others. The bocage leaves on the companion group are made in the same manner.

Figure 27.119. Shepherdess with lamb, shepherd with dog, a pair, with bocages. H: 7.2" (L), 7.7" (R). Note the full, crisp bocages. Price C.

Figure 27.120. Shepherdess with lamb, shepherd with dog, a pair, with bocages. H: ~7.2". Like the previous pair and perhaps from the same pot bank. Price C.

Figure 27.121. Shepherdess with lamb, with spill vase. H: 7.3". Price B. *Andrew Dando Antiques.*

Figure 27.122. Shepherdess with lamb, shepherd with dog, a pair, with spill vases. H: ~7". Price C. *Andrew Dando Antiques.*

Figure 27.123. Shepherd with dog, with spill vase. H: 6.9". Like the shepherd in the previous pair but the branch on the spill vase points to the other side. Price B. *Eileen and Robert Carde.*

Figure 27.124. Shepherd with dog and sheep, with bocage. L: ~7". Restoration of outer bocage fronds. Price B.

Figure 27.125. Shepherd, with sheep and squirrels, with bocage. L: ~7". Price B.

Figure 26.126. Shepherdess holding garland, with sheep, with vase. Impressed "NEALE & Co". H: ~8.5". Price B.

Figure 27.127. Shepherdess holding garland, with sheep, with vase. Impressed "NEALE & Co". H: 8.7". Like the previous example but the color palette is more typical of Neale. Price C. *Jonathan Horne.*

Figure 27.128. Shepherdess with dog holding sheep. Height not known. Note the pink luster decoration. Price A.

Figure 27.129. Shepherd holding sheep. H: 9.5". A color-glazed figure from these molds (with a different base) is recorded (Metropolitan Museum 1974.356.302). Price A. *Nick Burton.*

Figure 27.130. Shepherdess holding sheep, shepherd. H: 9.7" (L), 10" (R). The shepherd probably originally held a metal crook in his raised hand. Price B. *Aurea Carter Antiques.*

Figure 27.131. *Spanifh Shepherd*. Made by Ralph Wood; impressed "69". H: 9.2". Price B.

Figure 27.132. *Spanifh Shepherd,* reverse of previous figure, with "69" impressed on the back of the base. Ralph Wood's *Worshiper* also occurs impressed "69".

Figure 27.133. *Spanifh Shepherd*. Attributed to Ralph Wood. H: 8.4". Price B. *Image courtesy of The Potteries Museum & Art Gallery, Stoke-on-Trent, UK.*

Figure 27.134. Shepherdess holding sheep, shepherd holding dog, a classically attired pair, with candlesticks. H: ~9.7". A rare combination of classical and contemporary themes. An unpainted creamware candlestick with the man is recorded marked "NEALE & Co".[1] Price D. *Image courtesy of The Potteries Museum & Art Gallery, Stoke-on-Trent, UK.*

Figure 27.135. Shepherdess holding basket, with sheep. H: 7.6". Such shepherdesses are uncommon. Rare examples in under-glaze colors are recorded. All examples are made without bocages. Price B.

Figure 27.136. Shepherdess holding basket, reverse of previous figure.

Figure 27.137. Shepherdess holding basket, with sheep. H: 8.1". Like the previous shepherdess but with notable differences in the hat and the sheep. Price B. *Brighton and Hove Museums.*

Figure 27.138. Shepherdess holding basket, with sheep. H: 7.7". Like the previous figures but with a different sheep, bonnet, and basket. Price B. *Jonathan Horne.*

Figure 27.139. Boy with dog. H: 6.6". Probably made at Leeds. An unpainted figure from these molds impressed "LEEDS POTTERY" is at Temple Newsam House (16.205/47). Price A. *Brighton and Hove Museums.*

Figure 27.140. Boy with dog. Impressed "T Smith". A figure from the same molds and also marked "T. Smith" occurs on the same base as the girl in the following example; it is decorated in under-glaze colors. Price B.

Figure 27.141. Girl with lamb. H: 8.5". Price A. *Cynthia Bell Wolodkin, Golden Retriever Antiques.*

Figure 27.142. Girl with lamb. Impressed "WEDGWOOD". H: 7.2". Pairs with the following figure. Price A. *Michael Dace.*

Figure 27.143. Boy with dog. Impressed "WEDGWOOD". H: 7.5". Pairs with the previous figure. Price A. *Michael Dace*

Figure 27.144. Boy with dog, girl with lamb, a pair. Impressed "WEDGWOOD". H: 7.5". Price B. *Skinner, Inc.; www.skinnerinc.com.*

Figure 27.145. Shepherd with dog, with spill vase. Probably made by the Scottish east coast potteries. H: ~7.5". With under-glaze and some enamel colors. Pairs with the following shepherdess. Price B. *John Howard; www.antiquepottery.co.uk.*

Figure 27.146. Shepherdess with lamb, with spill vase. Probably made by the Scottish east coast potteries. H: 7.5". With under-glaze and some enamel colors. Pairs with the previous shepherd. Price B. *Peter Flemans.*

Figure 27.147. Shepherd and shepherdess each with a sheep, a pair, with bocages. Attributed to Blue Group. H: ~6.8". The painting is typical, and the bocage flowers confirm the attribution. Price C.

Figure 27.148. Shepherd with sheep, with bocage. Attributed to Blue Group. H: 7.2". The flowers on the bocage confirm the attribution. Companion to the following shepherdess. Price B. *John Howard; www.antiquepottery.co.uk.*

Figure 27.149. Shepherdess with sheep, with bocage. Attributed to Blue Group. H: 6.8". The flowers on the bocage and base confirm the attribution. Companion to the previous shepherd. Price B. *Brighton and Hove Museums.*

Figure 27.150. Shepherd and shepherdess each with a sheep, an assembled pair, with bocages. Attributed to Blue Group. H: ~6.8". The bocages are typical of Blue Group but are not specific to it. The similarity to previous examples supports the attribution. Price C.

Figure 27.151. Shepherd with sheep and dog, with bocage. H: 6". A fine example with the three-leaflet bocage fronds found on as-yet unclassified figures. Price B. *John Howard; www.antiquepottery.co.uk.*

Figure 27.152. Shepherd with sheep and dog, with bocage. H: 6". From the same pot bank as the previous example and having the same bocage fronds. Price B. *John Howard; www.antiquepottery.co.uk.*

Figure 27.153. Shepherdess with sheep, with spill vase. H: ~6". The leaf fronds are like those on the previous two examples, and all probably come from the same source. If formed with a bocage, this shepherdess would have been a companion subject to the previous shepherd. Price B.

Figure 27.154. Shepherd and shepherdess with sheep and a dog, with spill vase. Impressed "WALTON". H: 6.4". Price B.

Figure 27.155. Shepherd and shepherdess with sheep, with bocage. Impressed "WALTON". H: 7.6". Like the previous example but made without a dog and with a bocage rather than vase. Price B.

Figure 27.156. Shepherd and shepherdess, detail of previous example. The dog broke off the base in the biscuit firing, as evidenced by a rough patch and a paw that were glazed and painted at the time of manufacture.

Figure 27.157. Shepherd and shepherdess with a dog, sheep and goat, with bocage. Impressed "WALTON". H: ~7.6". Like the previous example but with a goat in place of one sheep. Price B.

Figure 27.158. Shepherd and shepherdess with sheep, with bocage. Impressed "WALTON". H: ~8". Like the previous example but with the figures reversed and a different array of animals and bocage. This anthemion bocage occurs infrequently on Walton examples. Price B.

Figure 27.159. Shepherd and shepherdess with sheep, with spill vase. Attributed to Ralph Wood; impressed "163" beneath. H: ~10.6". Price A.

Figure 27.160. Shepherd and shepherdess with sheep, with spill vase. Attributed to Ralph Wood. H: ~10.6". The rainbow-like colors on the base are typical of Ralph Wood. Price B.

Figure 27.161. Shepherd and shepherdess with sheep, with spill vase. Possibly by Ralph Wood. H: 10.6". Price B. *John Howard; www.antiquepottery.co.uk.*

Figure 27.162. Shepherd and shepherdess with sheep and dog, with spill vase. H: ~10.5". Unlike previous examples in that she wears a hat atop her bonnet, a dog is on the base, and birds with spread wings are on the spill vase. Price B. *Andrew Dando Antiques.*

Figure 27.163. A large spill vase with a shepherd and shepherdess accompanied by small sheep and a dog, flanked by two large sheep each with bocage. H: 9.5", L: 12.5". Groups of this form occur rarely with large sheep; examples with deer are more common. Price C. *Collection of Michael J. Smith.*

Figure 27.164. Shepherd with flock and dog within a walled circular enclosure, with a whimsical array of animals and a spill vase bedecked with a large snake. H: 9.5", L: 11". Shoddy modern reproductions of this fine group abound. Price E. *Image courtesy of The Potteries Museum & Art Gallery, Stoke-on-Trent, UK.*

Figure 27.165. Shepherd with flock and dog within a walled circular enclosure, with a whimsical array of animals and a spill vase bedecked with a large snake. H: 9". See figure 131.220 for a similar example without a shepherd. Price E. © *Christie's Images Limited 2013.*

Figure 27.166. Garniture comprising three spill vases, the central vase having a ram and goat with shepherd and dog, and the lateral vases each having a cow. Attributed to Dale. L: 9.4", H: 7.5" (center). The garniture is replete with Dale characteristics. The sheep and the shepherd occur as separate figures, also attributed to Dale. Price D, garniture. *Elinor Penna.*

Figure 27.167. Shepherd with dog, with ram and goat, with spill vase. Attributed to Dale. H: 7.5", L: 9.5". Like the spill vase in the previous garniture but decorated differently. Pairs with the following vase, and both have characteristic Dale features. Price D, pair. *The William Herbert and Nancy Hunt Collection.*

Figure 27.168. Shepherd with dog, with ram and ewe, with spill vase. Attributed to Dale. H: 7.5", L: 10". Pairs with the previous vase. Vases with jagged edged are typical of Dale, as are the twelve-petalled bocage flowers. Price D, pair. *The William Herbert and Nancy Hunt Collection.*

Figure 27.169. Detail of the previous base. The floral sprigs with pink and orange flowers are characteristic of Dale. *The William Herbert and Nancy Hunt Collection.*

28. Other Farm Workers

Figure 28.1. *Mower.* Gentleman holding scythe. Attributed to Ralph Wood; impressed "30". H: 7.5". This figure is porcelaneous. Made without bocage. Price B. *Aurea Carter Antiques.*

Figure 28.2. *Mower.* Gentleman holding scythe, with bocage. Attributed to Ralph Wood. H: 8". The font is larger than on the previous figure, but both styles are typical of Ralph Wood. Price B. *Image courtesy of The Potteries Museum & Art Gallery, Stoke-on-Trent, UK.*

Figure 28.3. *Mower*, reverse of previous figure. *Image courtesy of The Potteries Museum & Art Gallery, Stoke-on-Trent, UK.*

Figure 28.4. *Mower.* Gentleman holding scythe, with bocage. Attributed to Ralph Wood. H: 7.5". This tiny font occurs consistently on numbered Ralph Wood figures. Pairs with the following figure of a haymaker. Price B, pair. *Michael Goodacre.*

Figure 28.5. *Hay Maker.* Lady holding barrel. Attributed to Ralph Wood. H: 7.5". Pairs with the previous figure. On both bases, the painted line is on three sides only. Price B, pair. *Michael Goodacre.*

Figure 28.6. *Hay Maker.* Lady holding barrel. Attributed to Ralph Wood; impressed "33". H: 7.5". Made without bocage. There are traces of original gilding on her bodice and on the tree stump. Price B. *Elinor Penna.*

Figure 28.7. Lady holding barrel with "AlE" on it. Attributed to Ralph Wood; impressed "31". H: 7.5". Made without bocage. Price B.

Figure 28.8. *Hay Maker.* Lady holding barrel. Attributed to Ralph Wood; impressed "31". H: 7.5". Made without bocage. The head on this figure differs from that on the previous three hay maker figures, all by Ralph Wood. Price B. *Image courtesy of The Potteries Museum & Art Gallery, Stoke-on-Trent, UK.*

Figure 28.9. *Hay Maker*, reverse of previous figure. *Image courtesy of The Potteries Museum & Art Gallery, Stoke-on-Trent, UK.*

Figure 28.10. Gentleman holding scythe, with bocage. H: ~8". The bocage and rainbow painting on the mound are consistent with a Ralph Wood attribution, but the painted line bands all four sides of the base. The formation of the interior of the base is unknown. Price B. *Andrew Dando Antiques.*

Figure 28.11. Gentleman holding scythe, reverse of previous figure. *Andrew Dando Antiques.*

Figure 28.12. *Mower, Mate.* Gentleman holding scythe, lady holding barrel, a pair. Attributed to Dudson. H: 7.7". A Dudson x-sprig is to the left of her feet. The titling is typical of Dudson. Price B. *Bamfords Auctioneers and Valuers Ltd.*

Figure 28.13. Gentleman holding scythe. Possibly by Enoch Wood. H: 7.5". After the Ralph Wood *Mower* previously shown. Price A. *www.madelena.com.*

Figure 28.14. Lady holding a barrel. Attributed to Gray Base Group. H: 7.5". This figure may be a companion subject to the following figure, but she also portrays summer in a set of the four seasons attributable to this Group. Made without bocage. Price A.

Figure 28.15. Gentleman holding scythe, with bocage. Attributed to Gray Base Group. H: 7.5". Price A.

Figure 28.16. Gentleman holding scythe, with bocage. H: 7.5". The three-leaflet bocage fronds occur on an unclassified group of figures with shared features. Companion subject to the following example. Price A.

Figure 28.17. Lady holding barrel, with bocage. H: 7.5". With the same three-leaflet bocage fronds as the previous male figure, its companion subject. Price A. *Nicholas Frost Antiques.*

Figure 28.18. Gentleman holding scythe, lady holding barrel and basket, a pair, with bocages. Attributed to Leather Leaf Group. H: 7.4". The bocages and bases are characteristic of the Group. An uncommon true pair. Price C.

Figure 28.19. Gentleman holding scythe, lady holding barrel and basket, reverse of previous pair.

Figure 28.20. Lady holding barrel and basket, with bocage. Attributed to Leather Leaf Group. H: ~7.5". Bocage restored. Like the lady in the previous pair, but the base (specific to the Group) is painted differently. Price A.

Figure 28.21. Gentleman holding scythe, with bocage. Attributed to Leather Leaf Group. H: ~7.5". Bocage restored. Like the gentleman in the previous pair, but the base (specific to the Group) is painted with the particularly thick blue scrolls that this pot bank favored. Price A.

Figure 28.22. Gentleman holding scythe, with bocage. Attributed to Patriotic Group. H: 8.6". The holly bocage is specific to the Patriotic Group. Pairs with the following lady. Price C, pair.

Figure 28.23. Lady with rake, with bocage. Attributed to Patriotic Group. H: 8.8". Pairs with the previous gentleman. Price C, pair.

Figure 28.24. Lady with rake, reverse of previous figure. The holly berries are integral to the bocage leaves, and the same molds were used to form both sides of each leaf. The gentleman's bocage is made in the same way.

Figure 28.25. Gentleman holding scythe, lady with rake, a pair, with bocages. Attributed to Patriotic Group. H: ~8.7". Like the previous figures and from the same molds, but with different bocages and in a turquoise palette. Price C.

Figure 28.26. Gentleman and lady, each with sickle and wheat, a pair. H: 8.6" (L), 9" (R). Made without bocages. These figures are uncommon as a pair and are creamware. Their facial features are suggestive of Leeds. The bases are closed beneath. Price B.

Figure 28.27. Lady with sickle. H: 9". Price A.

Figure 28.28. Lady with sickle. H: 9". Price A. *Elinor Penna.*

Figure 28.29. Lady with rake, gentleman with sickle, with bocage. Probably made by Enoch Wood. H: ~10". This box base and bocage occur routinely on Enoch Wood figures. Price B.

Figure 28.30. Lady with rake, gentleman with sickle, with bocage. Probably made by Enoch Wood. H: 10". Like the previous example, but the base is painted differently. The bocage also differs, but it is typical of Enoch Wood. Price A. *Robert Hawker.*

Figure 28.31. Lady with rake, gentleman with sickle, with bocage. H: ~9.5". The bocage is restored. The figures are as in the previous two examples, but she now has a bonnet atop her cap. Price A.

Figure 28.32. Lady with rake, gentleman with sickle, with bocage. H: ~9.5". Price B.

Figure 28.33. Harvesters, a lady and gentleman, with ale barrel, with bocage. H: 10.1". Losses to objects in hands. Like the previous examples, but the figures now are enjoying ale and he holds a bag (possibly a money bag). Price B. *Brighton and Hove Museums.*

Figure 28.34. Harvester, lady with rake and jug, with bocage. Impressed "WALTON". H: ~6.2". Pairs with the following gentleman. Price A.

Figure 28.35. Harvester, gentleman with barrel, with bocage. Impressed "WALTON". H: 7.2". Pairs with the previous lady. Price A. *Peter Flemans.*

Figure 28.36. Gentleman and lady harvesters, she with basket, he with goblet and hoe, with rake, with bocage. Attributed to Box Title Group. H: 6.2". Pairs with a similarly styled gardening group, as in the next example. Price B.

Figure 28.37. Gentleman and lady gardeners, gentleman and lady harvesters, a pair of groups, with bocages. Attributed to Box Title Group. H: 6.2". The two-tone color palette on the bases is typical of the Box Title Group. Price C.

Figure 28.38. Milkmaid with yolk and pails. H: 6.3". The only known example. After a figure by the Imperial Porcelain Factory of St. Petersburg, circa 1817 (Victoria & Albert Museum c.59-1933). The pails are decorated in luster. The flowers at her feet are not inconsistent with an Enoch Wood attribution. Price C. © *Fitzwilliam Museum, Cambridge.*

Figure 28.39. Milkmaid with cow and farmer with cow, each with a bocage and flanking a spill vase. A small piper sits at the base of the vase, with swans at his feet. L: 10.5", H: 9.4". Price D. © *Fitzwilliam Museum, Cambridge.*

Figure 28.40. Two small cows each with a bocage, with a boy, girl, dog, and spill vase. H: ~9". The cows are smaller than those in the previous example. Both bocages are restored. Price A.

Figure 28.41. Large bull with a farmer. L: 16" at base. A large bull from the same molds occurs without a farmer and with an opening cut in its back, perhaps to accommodate a tradesman's sign (Vol. 3, fig. 118.1). Price E.

Figure 28.42. Cow with milkmaid. H: 7.8". Price C. *Elinor Penna.*

Figure 28.44. Milkmaid with cow and calf, detail of bocage on previous group. This bocage occurs on several figures awaiting classification. *Elinor Penna.*

Figure 28.43. Milkmaid with cow and calf, with bocage. H: 8.4", L: 9.8". A very unusual group. Price D. *Elinor Penna.*

Figure 28.45. Farmer with cow, calf, and dog, with spill vase. Attributed to Patriotic Group. H: 8.5". Other groups with this base and spill vase can be attributed to the Patriotic Group. "COW" is painted in red letters on the cow's back. Price B. *Bonhams.*

Figure 28.46. Cow with calf and milkmaid. H: 6". Figure groups of this form are more usually decorated in under-glaze colors. Price B. *John Howard; www.antiquepottery.co.uk.*

Figure 28.47. Farmer with cow and calf, with bocage. H: ~6.5". Bocage restored. Price A.

Figure 28.48. Milkmaid with cow, farmer with cow, a pair, with bocages. H: ~7.8". Price C.

Figure 28.49. Farmer with cow and calf, with bocage. H: 7.2". Bocage restored. Price A.

Figure 28.50. Farmer with cow, milkmaid with cow, a pair, with bocages. Attributed to Dudson. H: 5.3". The bocages are typical of Dudson. Price B. *K. Gomersall.*

Figure 28.51. Milkmaid with cow, with bocage. Attributed to Leather Leaf Group. H: ~7". The attribution is based on the two distinctive flowers on the base. The bocage is restored. Price A.

Figure 28.52. *MILK MAID* (impressed in front of base). Milkmaid standing with two cows and bocage. H: 6.5", L: 6.5". A rare group. The bocage and maid's head are restored. Price A.

Figure 28.53. Milkmaid standing with cow, with bocage. H: 4.7". Price B. *Andrew Dando Antiques.*

Figure 28.54. Milkmaid standing with cow, with bocage. H: ~4.7". Price B. *Andrew Dando Antiques.*

Figure 28.55. Milkmaid standing with cow, with bocage. H: 4.6". The bocage may be restored. Price A.

Figure 28.56. Milkmaid seated with cow, with bocage. H: ~4.6". Price B. *Collection of Susan and Richard Cann.*

Figure 28.57. Milkmaid seated with cow, reverse of previous example. *Collection of Susan and Richard Cann.*

Figure 28.58. Milkmaid seated with cow, with bocage. H: ~4.7". Price B.

Figure 28.59. Milkmaid seated with cow, with bocage. Attributed to Patriotic Group. H: ~4.8". Price A.

Figure 28.60. Milkmaid seated with cow, with bocage. Attributed to Patriotic Group. H: 4.8". Price B. *Elinor Penna.*

29. Trades and Occupations

Figure 29.1. Shoemaker and lady, hairdresser and lady, a pair, with bocages. Possibly made by Enoch Wood. H: ~6.7". The painting of the bases, the flowers on one base, and the leaves on the bocages suggest the attribution. After porcelain groups first issued by Derby in 1766, after Sèvres figures of 1756 that were modeled by Etienne-Maurice Falconet. Price B.

Figure 29.2. Hairdresser and lady, with bocage. Attributed to Patriotic Group. H: ~9". Pairs with the following shoemaker and lady. Price A. *Michael Goodacre.*

Figure 29.3. Detail of the floral sprigs on the base of the previous example. These sprigs are only recorded on Patriotic Group figures. *Michael Goodacre.*

Figure 29.4. Shoemaker and lady, with bocage. Attributed to Patriotic Group. H: ~9". Pairs with the previous hairdresser group and has the same bocage. Price A.

Figure 29.5. *SHOEMAKER & MATE.* Shoemaker and lady, with bocage. Attributed to Patriotic Group. H: ~9". Like the previous example but with a title on a tablet. Bocage largely restored. Price A.

Figure 29.6. Detail of the title tablet on the previous example. Titled Patriotic Group examples are often titled in this manner.

Figure 29.7. *BARBER & MATE.* Hairdresser and lady, with bocage. Attributed to Patriotic Group. H: 9". Like other Patriotic Group examples shown here, but with a titled tablet and cilantro bocage fronds. Price B.

Figure 29.8. Hairdresser and lady, with bocage. Attributed to Patriotic Group. H: ~9". The figures and base are as in the previous example. These bocage flowers are specific to the Patriotic Group. Pairs with the following example. Price B. *Andrew Dando Antiques.*

Figure 29.9. Shoemaker and lady, with bocage. Attributed to Patriotic Group. H: ~9". Pairs with the previous example. Price A.

Figure 29.10. Shoemaker and lady, hairdresser and lady, a pair, with bocages. Attributed to Patriotic Group. H: ~9". From the same molds as previous examples but with different bocages. The sprigs on the bases are specific to the Patriotic Group. Price B.

Figure 29.11. Hairdresser and lady, with bocage. Attributed to Patriotic Group. H: ~9". Like previous examples but with the holly bocage that is specific to the Patriotic Group. Price B.

Figure 29.12. Shoemaker and lady, with bocage. Attributed to Patriotic Group. H: ~9". Like previous examples but with a different and less common bocage. Characteristic sprigs are on the base. Price A. *Michael Goodacre.*

Figure 29.13. Shoemaker and lady, with bocage. H: ~9". The base, figures, and bocage differ from those used for previous examples on this theme, and there are no features to support attribution. Price A.

Figure 29.14. Shoemaker and lady, with bocage. H: ~9". Like the previous example but with a different bocage. Note the crude animals on the base, a feature not found on any of the previous examples of this subject. Price A.

Figure 29.15. Cobbler. Probably made by "Sherratt." H: ~4". This base occurs on other figures that link to "Sherratt," but this figure lacks features to support attribution. Price A.

Figure 29.16. Barber shaving a gentleman. H: 5.4". Price B. *Image courtesy of The Potteries Museum & Art Gallery, Stoke-on-Trent, UK.*

Figure 29.17. *DEP GOB BALD WIG THE LONDON BARBER* (impressed on plinth). Barber with a wig. H: 6.5". The wig is placed upside down. Price B. *Brighton and Hove Museums.*

Figure 29.18. *DEP GOBBLE WIG THE LONDON BARBER* (impressed on plinth). Barber with a wig. H: 6.4". Price B.

Figure 29.19. Barber with a wig. Attributed to "Sherratt." H: ~6.5". This base is specific to "Sherratt." Price B.

Figure 29.20. Barber with a wig. Possibly made by "Sherratt." H: 6.4". The figure is like the previous barber. The colors and painting of the waistcoat are consistent with "Sherratt," but the base is not. Price B. *Brighton and Hove Museums.*

Figure 29.21. Lady with a bunch of keys, possibly a landlady. H: 7.5". Price B. *Andrew Dando Antiques.*

Figure 29.22. *LAND LORD &, LANDLADY.* Attributed to "Sherratt." H: 7.5" (L), 7.2" (R). Known from only these examples. Typical "Sherratt" features include the bases, the titles, and her dress pattern. Possibly after an illustration of the landlord and landlady in Robert Burns's *Tam O'Shanter* (Vol. 2, fig. 37.8). Price F. *Brighton and Hove Museums.*

Figure 29.23. Barmaid holding a bottle. H: 7.6". Known as the "Bawdy Barmaid" because the figure often has an open hole between her legs. In this case, she has two well-modeled legs with a hole between, the area around the hole being painted to represent exaggerated genitalia. Price C.

Figure 29.24. Barmaid, reverse of previous figure.

Figure 29.25. Barmaid holding a bottle. Possibly made by Lakin & Poole. H: 8.8". The back of the base is unpainted. The palette and the mode of painting suggest the attribution. Price B. *Image courtesy of The Potteries Museum & Art Gallery, Stoke-on-Trent, UK.*

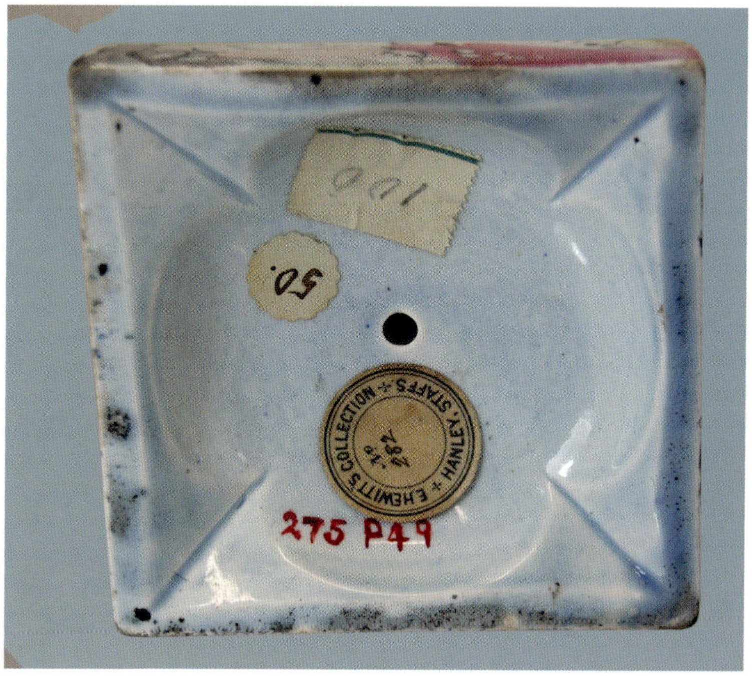

Figure 29.26. Barmaid, base of previous example. The corners are not inconsistent with a Lakin & Poole attribution, but the large clover-leaf impression is most unusual. *Image courtesy of The Potteries Museum & Art Gallery, Stoke-on-Trent, UK.*

Figure 29.27. *Dray Men.* Two dray men, one holding a tankard, with bocage. H: 9.5". Dray men were the brawny men who delivered 36-gallon beer kegs on horse-drawn carts called drays. Price D. *Brighton and Hove Museums.*

Figure 29.28. *Dray Men,* detail showing the inn sign on the previous example. Unlike most, this sign is original. *Brighton and Hove Museums.*

Figure 29.29. *Draymen*, by T. L. Busby for *Costumes of the Lower Orders of London*, published 1820. This print probably was the design source for the draymen groups shown here. *David Brass Rare Books Inc.*

Figure 29.30. *Dray Men.* Two dray men holding a tankard, with bocage. H: 9.5". Note the luster tankard. Made without an inn sign. These three-leaflet bocage fronds occur on an unclassified group of fine figures. Restoration to bocage on the left side. Price D.

Figure 29.31. Boy pushing a barrow with a beer keg. H: 4.5". The barrel possibly served as an inkwell. Price C.

Figure 29.32. Boy pushing a barrow with a beer keg. H: 5.5". The barrel is again formed to serve as an inkwell, but, unlike the previous example, there is a support beneath the barrel and the wheel lacks spokes. A reading maid occurs on this base (fig. 25.39). Price C.

Figure 29.33. Boy pushing a barrow with a beer keg. H: 4.8". There is a hole in the top of the barrel. Price C. *Collection of Michael J. Smith.*

Figure 29.34. Girl at the water pump. H: 6.4". Because milk was illegally diluted with water, the water pump was dubbed "the cow with the iron tail," the same name given this rare group. Also recorded on an oval base. After an engraving in William Henry Pyne's *Microcosm* (1803–1806). Price C.

Figure 29.35. Blacksmith at the anvil. H: 5.9". Pairs with the previous figure. Even rarer than "the cow with the iron tail." Price C.

Figure 29.36. Fisherwoman. Made by the Scottish east coast potteries. H: ~7.5". Decorated with enamel and underglaze colors. Price B. *John Howard; www.antiquepottery.co.uk.*

Figure 29.37. Scotsman drinking, fisherwoman, a pair. Made by the Scottish east coast potteries. H: 8.8". Figures of Faith, Hope and Charity also occur on this base (Vol. 2, fig. 92.55). Price B. *Andrew Dando Antiques.*

Figure 29.38. Scottish fisherwoman. H: 8.8". Price B. *Andrew Dando Antiques.*

Figure 29.39. *Spinning.* Attributed to Ralph Wood; impressed "71". H: ~8". Ralph Wood's male *Spanifh Dancer* also occurs impressed "71". Price A.

Figure 29.40. Sunday school teacher. H: 7.2". Sunday schools played a pivotal role in teaching the young to read, and the tome beneath the gentleman's arm is probably the Bible, which was the reading primer of its day. Price B.

Figure 29.41. Sunday school teacher. Possibly made by "Sherratt." H: 7.3". Similar bases occur on "Sherratt" figures, but this figure lacks other "Sherratt" features. Price B.

Figure 29.42. Town crier. H: 5.5". Scroll reads "LOST on the first day of last term, Lawyers conscience!! whoever finds the same & brings it to the Crier, will receive the handsome reward of six shillings & eight pence." A rare figure. Price B. *Brighton and Hove Museums.*

Figure 29.43. Town crier. H: ~6". Restoration to hands and possible loss of scroll. Price A.

Figure 29.44. Town crier. H: ~5". Price A.

Figure 29.45. Butcher. H: 6". The striped trousers and apron suggest this uncommon figure is a butcher, but it may portray the theatrical character Sam Swipes (Vol. 2, ch. 53). Price B. *John Howard; www.antiquepottery.co.uk.*

Figure 29.46. Laborer holding an axe and spade, a barrel and bag on his back. H: 5.9". Made without bocage. Price B. *Eileen and Robert Carde.*

Figure 29.47. *THE POOR LABORER.* Laborer holding an axe and spade. H: 6.2". Made without bocage. Like the previous figure but made without a bag and barrel on his back. Price B. *Eileen and Robert Carde.*

Figure 29.48. Two laborers, a comparison of the previous two figures. Only the man on the right has a barrel and bag on his back. *Eileen and Robert Carde.*

Figure 29.49. Chimney sweep. H: 7". This figure form was first manufactured to represent winter by Lunéville, after a model by Paul Louis Cyfflé. Examples attributed to Ralph Wood occur impressed "5", "6", or "74" and may be titled *Sloth* or *Clown*. Price A. *Andrew Dando Antiques.*

Figure 29.50. Chimney sweep and child, with donkey. H: 7.5". All examples of chimney sweeps shown here are rare and all were made without bocages. Price B. *Collection of Arnold and Barbara Berlin.*

Figure 29.51. Chimney sweep with child astride a donkey. H: ~6". Price B.

Figure 29.52. Chimney sweep astride a donkey. H: ~6". Uses molds from both previous examples, and all three figures may be from the same pot bank. Price B. *Andrew Dando Antiques.*

Figure 29.53. Chimney sweep astride a donkey, reverse of previous example. *Andrew Dando Antiques.*

Figure 29.54. Chimney sweep's wife and child astride a donkey, chimney sweep astride a donkey, a pair. H: 6". Known from only this pair. Price D. *The William Herbert and Nancy Hunt Collection.*

Figure 29.55. Gentleman with pack donkey and dog, with bocage. Attributed to Patriotic Group. H: 6.9". Known as "The Jolly Traveller" because some examples are titled thus. In the days before macadamized roads, pack animals transported wares across countryside impassable to wheeled traffic. Price C.

Figure 29.56. *Jolly Traveller, Jolly Traveller.* An assembled pair, each with man, pack donkey, dog, and bocage. Attributed to Patriotic Group. H: ~7". Like the previous example but paired and titled. Price C.

30. Vendors and People with Baskets

In the pre-Victorian era, vendors routinely peddled their goods and services on the streets. They loudly advertised anything and everything—from chair-mending to hot pies—by crying out the merits of their offerings. Sophisticated series of engravings of "London Cries" or the sight of vendors on village squares probably inspired some of the figures below. This was the era of child labor, so young children also hawked their wares. A host of small figures holding baskets reflect this theme. Cherubs and other figures holding baskets are shown in Volume 4, chapters 155 and 197.

Figure 30.1. Lady with a basket of flowers or produce. H: 11". Price B. *The William Herbert and Nancy Hunt Collection.*

Figure 30.2. Lady, reverse of previous figure. *The William Herbert and Nancy Hunt Collection.*

Figure 30.3. Girl with a fruit basket, boy with a pastry basket, a pair, with bocages. Impressed "WALTON". H: 6.8". Price B. *Michael Goodacre (L), Brighton and Hove Museums (R).*

Figure 30.4. Girl fruit vendor with angel wings, with a basket. Possibly made by Ralph Wood. H: ~7". Made without bocage. The line bands three sides of the base. Price A.

Figure 30.5. Boy with a pastry basket, girl with a fruit basket, a pair, with bocages. Attributed to Enoch Wood; both impressed "3" beneath. H: 7". Figures, bases, and bocages of these forms were excavated from the Burslem Old Town Hall site associated with Enoch Wood. Price B. *Collection of Michael J. Smith.*

Figure 30.6. Girl with a fruit basket, boy with a pastry basket, a pair. Possibly made by Enoch Wood. H: ~6.5". Made without bocages. The bases are in the style of Enoch Wood, and the figures are from the same molds as the previous pair. Price B.

Figure 30.7. Girl fruit vendor with angel wings, with a basket. Possibly made by Enoch Wood. H: 6.2". Made without bocage. Like the previous girl but the mound beneath her feet is now as wide as the base. Price A.

Figure 30.8. Boy vendor with a basket. H: 6.7". From the same figure molds as previous similar figures, but the base is painted in a most unusual manner. Made without bocage. Price A. *Andrew Dando Antiques.*

Figure 30.9. *BY A VACH.* Jewish watch vendor. H: 6.1". After earlier porcelain figures. Chelsea made the *Jewish Pedlar* circa 1750, adapted from Meissen's *Trinket-seller*. Derby followed with a pair of *Jewish Pedlars,* circa 1760. Price B. *Brighton and Hove Museums.*

Figure 30.10. Jewish watch seller. H: ~6.1". Price A.

Figure 30.11. "Marmot girl," girl holding a box with a piglet in it. Impressed "WEDGWOOD". H: 7.5". This figure of a girl with a piglet in a box is dubbed "the marmot girl." It is after a figure modeled by Paul Louis Cyfflé and made by Lunéville. Price A.

Figure 30.12. & *Partner*. "Marmot girl," girl holding a box with a piglet in it. Attributed to Ralph Wood. H: 8.5". Also occurs impressed "4", sometimes titled *Mate*. Price A. *Brighton and Hove Museums.*

Figure 30.13. "Marmot girl," girl holding a box with a piglet in it. H: 7.8". In French, a "marmotte" is a scarf tied under the chin, while a "marmot" is a bratty child, so the figure's naming results from butchering the French language. Price A. *Brighton and Hove Museums.*

Figure 30.14. "Dutch boy," boy holding a basket. Attributed to Ralph Wood. H: 6.5". Figures titled *Dutch Boy* and *Dutch Girl* are recorded in Wood ledgers. Falkner records this figure impressed "49". Price A. *K. Stafford.*

Figure 30.15. "Dutch girl," girl with a basket. Attributed to Ralph Wood; impressed "50". H: 6.5". Companion subject to the previous figure. Price A. *Aurea Carter Antiques.*

Figure 30.16. Broadside vendor, lady with dog, a pair. Attributed to Ralph Wood. H: 5.4". His broadsheet is inscribed "S. F. Burdill". Sir Francis Burdett (1770–1844), a popular radical reformer, was prominent from the late 1790s, so these figures were probably made by Ralph Wood III. Price A. *Michael Goodacre.*

Figure 30.17. Broadside vendor and lady with dog, reverse of previous pair. From beneath, the bases have rounded internal corners. *Michael Goodacre.*

Figure 30.18. Broadside vendor. H: 6.2". Inexpensive broadsides were the press of their day, and broadsides filled with salacious sagas were particularly popular. Price A.

Figure 30.19. *BALLAD SINGER* (poorly impressed on front edge of base). H: ~6". Ballad sellers sang the tunes of the ballads they wished to sell, as the title on this figure indicates. Price A.

Figure 30.20. Gentleman, lady broadside vendor, a pair. Attributed to Gray Base Group. H: ~6". The man possibly once held an object in his outstretched hand. The bases are a particularly yellow variation of the gray shade most commonly used by this pot bank. Price A.

Figure 30.21. Gentleman and lady, each holding a basket. H: ~9". Probably used for holding sweetmeats (small confections such as candied fruits, nuts, or flowers). Price A.

Figure 30.22. Gentleman and lady, each holding a basket. H: 8". Bocage lost. The girl's head and bodice different from those in the previous example. Price A. *Barbara Gair, www.castle-antiques.com.*

Figure 30.23. Gentleman and lady, each holding a basket. Probably made by Enoch Wood. H: 9". Bocage lost. On a typical Enoch Wood base. Price A. *Michael Goodacre.*

Figure 30.24. Boy beside baskets with rabbit and eggs, with bocage. Attributed to Straw Flower Group. H: 6". Straw Flower examples most commonly have these tiny bocage flowers (each with five cleft petals), and there is a hint of an impressed flower (dabbed yellow) on the base. Price A.

Figure 30.25. Boy beside baskets with rabbit and eggs, with bocage. Attributed to Enoch Wood. H: 6". The bocage and the figure match excavated Enoch Wood shards and figures. Price A. *The William Herbert and Nancy Hunt Collection.*

Figure 30.26. Reverse of the bocage on the previous figure. These seven-leaflet fern fronds are not specific to Enoch Wood, but they occur frequently on Enoch Wood figures. *The William Herbert and Nancy Hunt Collection.*

Figure 30.27. Boy beside baskets with rabbit and eggs. Probably made by Enoch Wood. H: 5.7". Made without bocage. The figure is like the previous figure, and its base is typical of Enoch Wood. Pairs with the following girl. Price A.

Figure 30.28. Girl with a basket atop her head. Probably made by Enoch Wood. H: 6.3". Made without bocage. Pairs with the previous boy. Perhaps after *The Strawberry Seller* in the *Cries of London* series, after paintings by Francis Wheatley. Price A.

Figure 30.29. Girl with a basket atop her head, with bocage. Probably made by Enoch Wood. H: 6.9". The base and bocage (largely restored) are in the style of Enoch Wood. Price A.

Figure 30.30. Lady holding a box with mice. Probably made by "Sherratt." H: 4.4". The pink luster on the box, base, and clothing is suggestive of "Sherratt," as are the cockade on the hat and the style of the figure. Made without bocage. Price A.

Figure 30.31. *LONDON CRYERS, LONDON CRYERS* (both titles impressed; her title concealed by the red line on the base). Gentleman with a bowl of produce, lady with a bowl of fruit, an assembled pair. Attributed to "Sherratt." H: 6.1". Made without bocages. The bases are specific to "Sherratt." Price B.

Figure 30.32. Lady with a bowl of fruit, with bocage. Attributed to "Sherratt." H: 6.1". Like the previous lady *LONDON CRYERS* but with a typical "Sherratt" bocage. Such figures are probably after one or other of the popular *Cries of London* prints. Price A.

Figure 30.33. Lady with a bowl of fruit, reverse of previous figure.

Figure 30.34. Gentleman and lady vendors each with a basket, a pair. Attributed to "Sherratt." H: 6.1" (L), 6.2" (R). Made without bocages. These bases are specific to "Sherratt." Price B.

Figure 30.35. Gentleman and lady vendors each with a basket, a pair, with bocages. Attributed to "Sherratt." H: 6" (L), 5.6" (R). Price A.

Figure 30.36. Lady vendor with a basket, with bocage. H: 5.5". Like the previous lady vendor but on a lower base and with a different bocage. Price A.

Figure 30.37. Lady and gentleman vendors each holding a box, a pair. Attributed to Patriotic Group. H: 6.2" (L), 6.1" (R). Made without bocages. Such bases are recorded only on Patriotic Group figures, and the painting is typical of the Group. Price B.

Figure 30.38. Gentleman vendor with a basket of oysters, with bocage (with losses). H: 5.5". Price A.

Figure 30.39. Gentleman vendor holding a bowl. H: 9.5". Bocage lost. The mate of this tall figure is as yet unrecorded. Price A.

Figure 30.40. Lady vendor holding a basket. H: 5.5". Bocage lost. Price A. *Paul Andrews, Arundel, England.*

Figure 30.41. Gentleman vendor with a basket atop his head, with bocage. Probably attributable to Leather Leaf Group. H: 7.3". The leaves are very suggestive of the attribution, but the bocage flower is non-specific. Price A. *Brighton and Hove Museums.*

Figure 30.42. Gentleman vendor with a basket atop his head, with bocage. H: ~7.3". Bocage fronds on the left are restored. Price A.

Figure 30.43. Gentleman vendor holding a basket, with bocage. Attributed to Leather Leaf Group. H: ~6". The bocage flowers confirm the attribution. Price A.

Figure 30.44. Lady holding a large basket, with bocage. Probably made by Enoch Wood. H: ~7". The base and bocage are in the style of Enoch Wood. Price A.

Figure 30.45. Lady holding a large basket. Possibly made by Enoch Wood. H: 6.2". Bocage lost. The decoration of the base suggests the attribution. Price A. *Peter Flemans.*

Figure 30.46. Lady holding a basket, with bocage. H: ~6". Price A.

Figure 30.47. Gentleman fruit vendor holding a basket. H: 6.2". Made without bocage. Price A.

Figure 30.48. Gentleman fruit vendor holding a basket. H: ~5.5". Made without bocage. Price A.

Figure 30.49. Lady vendor holding a basket of fish. H: ~5.5". Made without bocage. Price A.

Figure 30.50. Lady holding a basket. H: 6". Made without bocage. Price A. *Brighton and Hove Museums.*

Figure 30.51. Lady holding a basket. H: ~5.7". Made without bocage. Price A.

Figure 30.52. Lady holding a basket. H: 5.7". Made without bocage. Like the previous figure but without a bonnet atop her cap. Price A.

Figure 30.53. Boy vendor holding a basket. H: 5.8". Price A. *Jack Hardin.*

Figure 30.54. Boy vendor holding fruit. H: 5.7". This vendor's garb leaves his knees exposed. Price A. *Aurea Carter Antiques.*

Figure 30.55. Boy vendor holding flowers. H: 5.7". From many of the same molds as the previous figure but painted with flowers rather than fruit. Price A.

Figure 30.56. Boy vendor holding a basket, with bocage. H: ~5". Price A.

Figure 30.57. Boy vendor holding a basket, with bocage. Attributed to Patriotic Group. H: 4.7". The uncommon base is as on figure 197.41 (Vol. 4). The bocage fronds (six-leaflets) and flowers are as might be expected. Price A.

Figure 30.58. Boy vendor, detail of the reverse of the bocage on the previous figure. This bocage occurs on other small Patriotic Group figures.

Figure 30.59. Boy vendor holding fruit, with bocage. H: ~5". Price A.

Figure 30.60. *FRUITBOYS.* Boy vendor holding a basket, with bocage. Attributed to Patriotic Group. H: 5.5". The bocage flowers are particular to the Patriotic Group. Price A.

Figure 30.61. *FRUITBOYS.* Boy vendor holding a basket, with bocage. Attributed to Patriotic Group. H: 5.7". Price A. *Mary and Maurice Norton.*

Figure 30.62. *FRUTEGIRL.* Girl vendor holding a basket, with bocage. Probably attributable to Box Title Group. H: 6". The title is typical as are the glazes and enamels. Price A.

Figure 30.63. Lady vendor holding a basket, with bocage. H: 5.5". Price A. *Brighton and Hove Museums.*

Figure 30.64. Boy vendor holding a basket, with bocage. H: ~5.3". Price A.

Figure 30.65. Boy vendor holding a basket, with bocage. H: ~5.5". Like the previous figure but with different bocage fronds. Price A.

Figure 30.66. Boy vendor holding a basket, with bocage. H: 5.5". From the same molds as the previous two figures, but note the huge fruit and different bocage. Price A.

Figure 30.67. Flower vendor dressed as a Turk, with a flower basket. H: ~4.6". Several other small figures modeled as Turks occur in this style and on this base. All are made without bocages. Price A.

Figure 30.68. Lady flower vendor. H: 4.4". Made without bocage. Price A. *Brighton and Hove Museums.*

Figure 30.69. Lady and gentleman vendors each with a basket, an assembled pair. H: 6". Price B. *Photograph Courtesy of Sotheby's, Inc. © 2013.*

Figure 30.70. Girl with a basket seated to the left. L: ~3.5". Made without bocage. Price A.

Figure 30.71. Putto with a basket seated to the right, girl with basket seated to the left, a pair. H: ~3.7", L: 3". Made without bocages. Price A. *Elinor Penna.*

Figure 30.72. Putto with a basket seated to the right, with bocage. Possibly made by Enoch Wood. H: ~4.2". The bocage and base are in the style of Enoch Wood. Price A.

Figure 30.73. Girl with a basket seated to the right, with bocage. Possibly made by Enoch Wood. H: ~4.2". The bocage and base suggest the attribution. Price A.

Figure 30.74. Girl with a basket seated to the right. Probably made by Enoch Wood. H: 3.3". Bocage lost. Like the previous figure. A painter's mark and "14" are impressed twice beneath. Numbers and marks like these are associated with Enoch Wood figures. Price A.

Figure 30.75. Girl with a basket seated to the right, with bocage. H: ~4.2". Price A.

Figure 30.76. Girl with a basket seated to the right. H: 3.7". Bocage probably lost. Price A.

Figure 30.77. Girl with a cornucopia seated to the left, with bocage. Attributed to Dale. H: ~4.2". These bocage flowers are only otherwise known from figures linked to Dale and from three marked Tittensor figures. Price A.

Figure 30.78. Girl with a basket seated to the left, with bocage. Attributed to Leaf Mat Group. H: ~4.2". Price A.

Figure 30.79. Girl with a basket seated to the left, with bocage. Attributed to Leaf Mat Group. H: ~4.2". The unusual cluster of four flowers is also on the bocage of a large bull attributed to the same Group. Price A.

Figure 30.80. Girl with a basket seated to the left, with bocage. Attributed to "Sherratt." H: 4.4". Sherratt made such small figures facing left and right, to pair. Three different heads occur on the left of the pair and two on the right. This example has a small round head. Price A.

Figure 30.81. Girl with a basket seated to the left, with bocage. Attributed to "Sherratt." H: ~4.4". Like the previous figure but with a larger head with puffy hair. This bocage occurs frequently on small "Sherratt" figures. Price A.

Figure 30.82. Girl with a basket seated to the left, with bocage. Attributed to "Sherratt." H: ~4.4". Like the previous figure, having the same head with puffy hair. The bocage flowers are different but occur often on small "Sherratt" figures. Price A.

Figure 30.83. Girl with a basket seated to the left, with bocage. Attributed to "Sherratt." H: ~4.4". The figure is like previous "Sherratt" figures but exhibits a third type of head. Companion to figure 30.89. Price A.

Figure 30.84. Girl with a basket seated to the right, with bocage. Attributed to "Sherratt." H: ~4.4". The same type of small round head as on figure 30.80. Small figures of this type facing right are recorded with two head forms, while examples facing left have three possible head forms. Price A.

Figure 30.85. Girl with a basket seated to the right, with bocage. Attributed to "Sherratt." H: ~4.4". Like the previous figure but with luster decoration, as occurs on some "Sherratt" figures. Price A.

Figure 30.86. Girl with a basket seated to the right, with bocage. Attributed to "Sherratt." H: ~4.4". The figure is like the previous two figures, but the head is different. Note the typical "Sherratt" anthemion bocage and dress pattern. Price A.

Figure 30.87. Girl with a basket seated to the right, with bocage. Attributed to "Sherratt." H: ~4.4". Like the previous figure but with a different typical "Sherratt" bocage. Price A.

Figure 30.88. Girl with a basket seated to the right, with bocage. Possibly attributable to "Sherratt". H: 3.9". Like previous "Sherratt" figures. "Sherratt" used these five-leaflet bocage fronds and these flowers (usually in three colors), but their combination is not otherwise recorded on "Sherratt" figures. Price A. *Michael Goodacre.*

Figure 30.89. Girl with a basket seated to the right, with bocage. Attributed to "Sherratt." H: 4.5". A companion to figure 30.83. A solid blue dress is atypical for "Sherratt" but is recorded. Price A. *Barbara Gair, www.castle-antiques.com.*

Figure 30.90. Girl with a basket, with bocage. Attributed to "Sherratt." H: ~4.7". The floral sprigs applied to either side of the base are characteristic of "Sherratt." Price A.

Figure 30.91. Girl with a basket seated to the left, with bocage. Attributed to Blue Group. H: ~4.4". The bocage fronds are specific to this Group. They are unpainted on the reverse. Price A.

Figure 30.92. Girl with a basket seated to the left, with bocage. Probably attributable to Blue Group. H: ~4.4". The same base and figure molds as the previous figure. The bocage leaves are not of a typical Blue Group form, but their painting style is. The dress pattern matches that on the following figure. Price A.

Figure 30.93. Girl with a basket seated to the right, with bocage. Attributed to Blue Group. H: ~4.5". Price A.

Figure 30.94. Reverse of bocage on previous figure. The fern-leaflet bocage fronds (with two leaflets and two flower stalks added to the mid-line of each) are specific to the Blue Group.

Figure 30.95. Girl with a basket seated to the right, with spill vase. H: 5.5". Price A. *Peter Flemans.*

Figure 30.96. Girl with a basket seated to the right, with spill vase with birds in the branches. H: 4.5". Price A. *The William Herbert and Nancy Hunt Collection.*

Notes

1. John Dale

1. The Dale family tree has been reconstructed from wills of Joshua, William, and John Dale (potter), the *Staffordshire Advertiser*, and trade directories.

2. Dudson Family

1. Audrey M. Dudson and Alison Morgan. *Dudson Staffordshire Figures*. (Stoke-on-Trent: Dudson Publications, 2006), 9
2. Ibid, 10.
3. The bocage shard is lost, but Malcolm Hodkinson photographed it when it was in Audrey Dudson's possession. Illustrated in figure 2.2 and as a line drawing in *Dudson Staffordshire Figures*, 11.
4. The author acknowledges Malcolm Hodkinson's development of this hypothesis.

3. Edge & Grocott

1. Reginald Haggar. *Staffordshire Chimney Ornaments*. (London: Phoenix House, 1955), 79.
2. Pat Halfpenny. English Earthenware Figures 1780–1840. (Woodbridge, Suffolk: Antique Collectors' Club, 1991), 245.

4. Samuel Hall

1. New Hall Street and Marsh Street join at a right-angle, so possibly the pot works occupied the corner site.
2. Haggar, *Staffordshire Chimney Ornaments*, 70.
3. Rodney Hampson. *Pottery References in the Staffordshire Advertiser, 1795–1865*. (Hanley: Northern Ceramic Society, 2000), 55.

5. Lakin & Poole

1. Haggar, *Staffordshire Chimney Ornaments*, 58.
2. Haggar, *Staffordshire Chimney Ornaments*, 58–59.
3. Llewellynn Jewitt. *The Wedgwoods: being a life of Josiah Wedgwood; with notices of his works and their productions, memoirs of the Wedgewood and other families, and a history of the early potteries of Staffordshire*. (London: Virtue, 1865), 251.
4. Ibid, 251.
5. Hampson, *Pottery References*, 92.
6. Ibid, 70–71.
7. Jewitt, *Ceramic Art of Great Britain*, 252.
8. Bonhams Knowle, March 1, 2005, lot 109.
9. Christie's South Kensington, June 11 1992, lot 94. Untitled and described as "on a purple square base."
10. John Hall. *Staffordshire Portrait Figures*. (New York: World Pub., 1972), 27, for the unmarked figure titled Ariadne. The similar marked but untitled figure is in the collection of the Fitzwilliam Museum, C.943-1928 and is shown in this work.

6. Leeds Pottery

1. Peter Walton. *Creamware and Other English Pottery at Temple Newsam House, Leeds*. (Bradford, U.K.: Manningham, 1976), 280.

7. Neale & Co. and Wilson

1. Peter Roden. *Copyhold Potworks and Housing in the Staffordshire Potteries, 1700–1832*. (Cumbria: Wood Broughton Publications, 2008), 33, 85.
2. Diana Edwards. *Neale Pottery and Porcelain, its Predecessors and Successors 1763–1829*. (London: Barrie & Jenkins, 1987), 43.
3. Ibid, 43.
4. Ibid. 154–5. Also Bonhams New Bond Street, April 14 2010, lot 10, creamware ladle impressed "Neale & Wilson".
5. Roden, *Copyhold Potworks and Housing*, 34.
6. *London Gazette*, Issue 13418, May 19, 1792, 4.
7. Hampson, *Pottery References*, 129.
8. Roden, *Copyhold Potworks and Housing*, 35.
9. Diana Edwards and Rodney Hampson. *English Dry-Bodied Stoneware: Wedgwood and Contemporary Manufacturers 1774–1830*. (Woodbridge, Suffolk: Antique Collectors' Club, 1998), 159.
10. Edwards, *Neale Pottery and Porcelain*, 178.

8. Ralph Salt

1. Hampson, *Pottery References*, 102.
2. Roden, *Copyhold Potworks and Housing*, 256.
3. Hampson, *Pottery References*, 102.
4. Ibid.

9. Theophilus Smith

1. J. F. Hughes. *Recollections of Old Liverpool by a Nonagerian*. (Liverpool, 1836), 100–103.
2. Hampson, *Pottery References*, 108.

10. Charles Tittensor

1. Hampson, *Pottery References*, 92.
2. Halfpenny, *English Earthenware Figures*, 111.
3. Ibid.

11. John Walton

1. Haggar, *Staffordshire Chimney Ornaments*, 72.
2. Ibid, 71.
3. Hampson, *Pottery References*, 63.
4. Roden, *Copyhold Potworks and Housing*, 308, 320.
5. Ibid, 258.
6. Myrna Schkolne. "A Pearlware Puzzle: Walton Figures and Their Look-Alikes," *American Ceramic Circle Journal*, Volume XVI (2011), 56–77.

12. Ralph Wedgwood

1. Edwards and Hampson, *English Dry-bodied Stoneware*, 195.
2. Ibid, 196.
3. Ibid.
4. Ibid, 197.
5. Jewitt, *The Wedgwoods*, 180.

13. Enoch Wood and Wood & Caldwell

1. Falkner, *Wood Family of Burslem*, 38.
2. Document PMI/1/70 in the Enoch Wood archive acquired by the Potteries Museum in 2005.
3. James Caldwell's diary, at www.jjhc.info/caldwelljames1770_1808.htm
4. Edwards and Hampson, *English Dry-bodied Stoneware*, 200.
5. John Ward. *The Borough of Stoke-upon-Trent*. (London: Lewis, 1843), 264.
6. Herbert Read. *Staffordshire Pottery Figures*. (London: Duckworth, 1929), plate 49.
7. The busts are in the Wisbech & Fenland Museum and, unlike most others with this mark, do not appear to be later reproductions.
8. An excavated figure of Prudence from the St. Paul's Church site associated with Enoch Wood production circa 1828 matches figures of Prudence marked "E. WOOD" and made decades earlier. Also, a partial figure of Falstaff excavated from the Burslem Town Hall site of the 1820s matches earlier figures marked "WOOD & CALDWELL".
9. The shards are now in The Potteries Museum and Art Gallery, Stoke-on-Trent.

14. Ralph Wood II and Ralph Wood III

1. The Big House Hiring Book at the Potteries Museum, as noted in Halfpenny, *English Earthenware Figures,* 70.
2. Wynne Hamilton-Foyn. "Who Modelled and Made Ralph Wood Figures?" Unpublished research, 2009. Copies at the Victoria and Albert Museum, British Museum, Potteries Museum, 8.
3. Ibid, 10.
4. Ibid, 11, 12.
5. Ibid, 4.
6. The incised mark "R. WOOD 1794" is found on enamel-painted figures of the Vicar and Moses, after the figure impressed "62" or "63". These examples are titled *VICAR AND MOSES,* with the "S" reversed and are probably Victorian or later. The Powerhouse Museum, Australia, has an example that was donated in 1927.
7. *Lost Sheep Found, Lost Piece Found, Scuffle, Tenderness, Friendship, Rural Pastime, Fortune,* a seated shepherd, a boy with birds' nests, and Chaucer (untitled) are recorded with this mark.
8. Enoch Wood figures sometimes also use impressed numbers. Although their modeling and enameling is very unlike that of Ralph Wood figures, past authors have incorrectly attributed Enoch Wood figures with numbers to Ralph Wood.
9. Exceptions are noted. A figure titled *Fortune*, with "W" impressed on the reverse, a pair of gardeners (figs. 24.115–117), and figure titled *Old Age*, with bocage, are confidently attributed to Ralph Wood, but all have the underneath of the base shaped as a squared recess.
10. One exception, a titled figure of *Fortune*, has been recorded with lines around all four sides of the base.
11. A figure titled *Charity* in the small red script used by Ralph Wood bears the impressed mark of Theophilus Smith. The figure exhibits no other Ralph Wood features.
12. The figures are impressed "169" and "170". These are the highest numbers used by Ralph Wood. If numbers did indeed correspond to the sequential introduction of figures, these figures would be of a slightly later date than most, and thus more likely to have larger bocages.
13. Blue is a very uncommon color for the line banding the base of earthenware figures. Blue banding has been noted on the pediment bases of an earthenware figure of St. Peter attributed to Ralph Wood.
14. The following examples on the list are known only from Frank Falkner's list published in *The Wood Family of Burslem* in 1912: 8 (gardener), 19, 21 (Venus), 22, 23, 33 (bull baiting), 49, 55, 62, 67 (girl with pitcher), 74, 81, 82 (bust of a divine), 96 (boy), 118, 119 (St. John), 123, 127, 135 (Cymon), 136 (Iphigenia), 169 (Fortune). The author has noted unnumbered examples of many of these figures.
15. Jupiter with an eagle to the right occurs impressed "29" and decorated in colored glazes, and an unnumbered enamel-painted version is recorded in Volume 4 of this work.

15. Other Makers' Marks

1. A. J. B Kiddell. "William Absolon of Yarmouth," *English Ceramic Circle Transactions*, 5:1 (1960), 55.
2. Ibid, 57.
3. British Museum AN9656290001.
4. Kiddell, *William Absolon*, plate 60.
5. Ibid, 62.
6. Ibid, plate 61.
7. Alwyn and Angela Cox. *Rockingham 1745–1842.* (Woodbridge, Suffolk: Antique Collectors' Club, 2001), 115.
8. Haggar, *Staffordshire Chimney Ornaments,* plate 46.
9. The *London Gazette* of December 24, 1818, announces the formation of this partnership. "Notice is hereby given, that the Partnership heretofore subsisting between us, John Phillips, Robert Dixon, William Austin, and Thomas Henderson, as Manufacturers of Earthenware, at Sunderland near the Sea, in the County of Durham, under the stile or firm of Dixon, Austin, Phillips and Co, the Sunderland Pottery, is this day dissolved by mutual consent, so far as regards the said John Phillips; and that the business will in future be carried on by us the undersigned, Robert Dixon, William Austin, and Thomas Henderson alone, in Partnership, at Sunderland aforesaid, under the stile or firm of Dixon, Austin, and Co. the Sunderland Pottery. As witness our hands this 17th day of December 1818." The author thanks Stephen Smith for sharing the information.
10. The *London Gazette* of January 7, 1840, announces the dissolution of "the firm of Dixon, Austin, and Company," effective December 31, 1839. The partners signing the notice are Robert Dixon, William Austin, and Alexander Phillips.
11. Haggar, *Staffordshire Chimney Ornaments,* plate 36.
12. The author thanks John Howard for this information.
13. Read, *Staffordshire Pottery Figures,* plate 60.
14. Edwards and Hampson, *English Dry-bodied Stoneware,* 179.

18. Brown Base Group

1. Only one Brown Base figure lacking cut internal corners has been noted. It portrays Leda and the Swan, and virtually identical examples with cut internal corners have been observed.

20. Patriotic Group

1. Halfpenny, *English Earthenware Figures*, 257.

21. "Sherratt" Group

1. H. M. Hodkinson and Judith Hodkinson. *Sherratt? A Natural Family of Staffordshire Figures.* (London: Chisquare, 1991).
2. Ibid.
3. Halfpenny, *English Earthenware Figures*, 263.
4. Hodkinson named this flower form.

22. Tunstall Group

1. The shards are now at The Potteries Museum, Hanley.
2. www.thepotteries.org/works/tunstall/highgate_potteries.htm.
3. Hampson, *Pottery References*, 63.
4. The name is spelled "Tunnicliff" or Tunicliff" in directories of 1835 and 1841.
5. Hampson, *Pottery References*, 54.
6. At quick glance, this flower is rather like a distinctive Patriotic flower. However, the Patriotic flower is larger and less compact, and its center is demarcated differently.

23. Other Groups

1. The author thanks Malcolm Hodkinson for this observation.

27. Shepherds and Shepherdesses

1. Edwards, *Neale Pottery and Porcelain*, plate X.

Bibliography

Bradshaw, Peter. *18th Century English Porcelain Figures.* Woodbridge, Suffolk: Antique Collectors' Club, 1981.

_____. *Derby Porcelain Figures 1750–1848.* London: Faber & Faber, 1990.

Cox, Alwyn and Angela Cox. *Rockingham 1745–1842.* Woodbridge, Suffolk: Antique Collectors' Club, 2001.

Dudson, Audrey M. and Alison Morgan. *Dudson Staffordshire Figures.* Stoke-on-Trent: Dudson Publications, 2006.

Earle, Cyril. *The Earle Collection of Early Staffordshire Pottery.* London: Brown, 1915.

Edwards Diana. *Neale Pottery and Porcelain, its Predecessors and Successors 1763–1829.* London: Barrie & Jenkins 1987.

Edwards, Diana and Rodney Hampson. *English Dry-Bodied Stoneware: Wedgwood and Contemporary Manufacturers 1774–1830.* Woodbridge, Suffolk: Antique Collectors' Club, 1998.

Falkner, Frank. *The Wood Family of Burslem.* London: Chapman & Hall, 1912.

Godden, Geoffrey A. *Encyclopaedia of British Pottery and Porcelain Marks.* London: Barrie & Jenkins, 1991.

Goodacre, J.M. *A Catalogue of the Goodacre Collection of Early Staffordshire Pottery Figures.* N.p.: Goodacre, 2007.

Grigsby, Leslie. *English Pottery 1650–1800: The Henry K. Weldon Collection.* London: Sotheby's Publications, 1990.

Haggar, Reginald. *Staffordshire Chimney Ornaments.* London: Phoenix House, 1955.

Halfpenny, Pat. *English Earthenware Figures 1780–1840.* Woodbridge, Suffolk: Antique Collectors' Club, 1991.

Halfpenny, Patricia and Stella Beddoe. *Circus and Sport.* Louisville, KY: J.B. Speed Art Museum, 1990.

Hall, John. *Staffordshire Portrait Figures.* New York: World Pub., 1972.

Hamilton-Foyn, Wynne. "Who Modelled and Made Ralph Wood Figures?" Unpublished research, 2009. Copies at the Victoria and Albert Museum, British Museum, Potteries Museum, Fitzwilliam Museum, Ashmolean Museum, and Wedgwood Museum.

Hampson, Rodney. *Pottery References in the Staffordshire Advertiser, 1795–1865.* Hanley: Northern Ceramic Society, 2000.

Hayden, Arthur. *Chats on English Earthenware.* London: Unwin, 1909.

Henrywood, R. K. *Staffordshire Potters 1781–1900.* Woodbridge: Antique Collectors' Club, 2002.

Hodkinson, H. M. and Judith Hodkinson. *Sherratt? A Natural Family of Staffordshire Figures.* London: Chisquare, 1991.

Horne, Jonathan. *A Collection of Early English Pottery, parts I to X 1981–1990.* London: Jonathan Horne, 1981–1990.

_____. *A Collection of Early English Pottery, parts XI to XX 1991–2000.* London: Jonathan Horne, 1991–2000.

Hughes, J. F. *Recollections of Old Liverpool by a Nonagerian.* Liverpool, 1836.

Jewitt, Llewellynn. *The Wedgwoods: being a life of Josiah Wedgwood; with notices of his works and their productions, memoirs of the Wedgewood and other families, and a history of the early potteries of Staffordshire.* London: Virtue., 1865.

Jewitt, Llewellynn. *The Ceramic Art of Great Britain.* N.p: Virtue, 1878.

Kiddell, A. J. B. "William Absolon of Yarmouth," *English Ceramic Circle Transactions*, 5:1, 1960, 53–64.

John, W. D., and Warren Baker. *Old English Lustre Ware.* New York: Walker, 1966.

Lewis, Griselda. *A Collector's History of English Pottery.* Woodbridge, Suffolk: Antique Collectors' Club, 1985.

Lewis, John, and Griselda Lewis. *Pratt Ware: English and Scottish Relief Decorated and Underglaze Coloured Earthenware.* Woodbridge, Suffolk: Antique Collectors' Club, 2006.

Locket, T. A. and P. A. Halfpenny, eds. *Creamware and Pearlware Re-Examined.* Stoke-on-Trent, City Museum and Art Gallery, 1989.

Manheim, Emily. Selections from the Hope McCormick Collection of Staffordshire Pottery. (Chicago, 1980).

McVeigh, Patrick. *Scottish East Coast Potteries.* Edinburgh: Donald, 1979.

Oliver, Anthony. *Staffordshire Pottery: the Tribal Art of England.* London: Heinemann, 1981.

Poole, Julia. *Plagiarism Personified.* Cambridge: Fitzwilliam Museum, 1986.

Pugh, P. D. Gordon. *Staffordshire Portrait Figures of the Victorian Age.* Woodbridge, Suffolk: Antique Collectors' Club, 1987.

Rackham, Bernard. *Catalogue of the Glaisher Collection of Pottery & Porcelain in the Fitzwilliam Museum, Cambridge.* Woodbridge, Suffolk: Antique Collectors' Club, 1987.

Read, Herbert. *Staffordshire Pottery Figures.* London: Duckworth, 1929.

Roden, Peter. *Copyhold Potworks and Housing in the Staffordshire Potteries, 1700–1832.* Cumbria: Wood Broughton Publications, 2008.

Schkolne, Myrna. "A Pearlware Puzzle: Walton Figures and Their Look-Alikes," *American Ceramic Circle Journal*, XVI (2011), 56–77.

_____. *People, Passions, Pastimes, and Pleasures: Staffordshire Figures 1810–1835.* Winston-Salem, NC: Hot Lane Press, 2006.

_____. "Ralph Wood's Enamel-painted Figures and Busts," *English Ceramic Circle Transactions*, 22 (2012), forthcoming.

Stanley, Louis T. *Collecting Staffordshire Pottery.* New York: Doubleday, 1963.

Staffordshire Education Dept. *A Directory of the Staffordshire Potteries.* Stafford: Staffordshire County Council, 1982.

Ward, John. *The Borough of Stoke-upon-Trent.* London: Lewis, 1843.

Walton, Peter. *Creamware and Other English Pottery at Temple Newsam House, Leeds.* Bradford, UK, Manningham, 1976.

Williams, Peter, and Pat Halfpenny. *A Passion for Pottery.* New York: Sotheby's, 2000.

Index

Italics denote titled figures